AF588425

THE ADAPTABILITY ADVANTAGE

JOHN SANEI

THE ADAPTABILITY ADVANTAGE

UNLEARN THE PAST
REWIRE YOUR AWARENESS
ELEVATE YOUR FUTURE

WILEY

Registered Office(s)

John Wiley & Sons, Inc., 111 River Street, Hoboken, NJ 07030, USA

John Wiley & Sons Ltd, New Era House, 8 Oldlands Way, Bognor Regis, West Sussex, PO22 9NQ, UK

John Wiley & Sons Singapore Pte. Ltd, 134 Jurong Gateway Road, #04-307H, Singapore 600134

For details of our global editorial offices, customer services, and more information about Wiley products visit us at www.wiley.com.

The manufacturer's authorized representative according to the EU General Product Safety Regulation is Wiley-VCH GmbH, Boschstr. 12, 69469 Weinheim, Germany, e-mail: Product_Safety@wiley.com.

Wiley also publishes its books in a variety of electronic formats and by print-on-demand. Some content that appears in standard print versions of this book may not be available in other formats.

Library of Congress Cataloging-in-Publication Data is Available:

ISBN 9781394421886 (Cloth)
ISBN 9781394421893 (ePub)
ISBN 9781394421909 (ePDF)

Cover Design: Wiley
Cover Images: © Kobee/Shutterstock, © TWINS DESIGN STUDIO/Shutterstock
Author Photo: © John Sanei

Set in 12/16 pts and Bembo Std by Straive, Chennai, India.

Printed and bound by CPI Group (UK) Ltd, Croydon, CR0 4YY

C9781394421886_120626

Contents

Preface

I want to begin by telling you a story that, in many ways, sits underneath everything that follows in this book, because it was the moment I realised that the greatest threat to any future we are trying to build is not a lack of intelligence or effort or even strategy but our attachment to whom we believe we are.

In 2008, I found myself sitting in the ruins of what had been, only 18 months earlier, a thriving small restaurant group. At one point there had been five locations across South Africa, a sense of momentum that felt unstoppable, and a life that, from the outside at least, looked like the natural reward for hard work and ambition. What I did not see at the time was that I had slowly wrapped my entire identity around that version of success and that, in doing so, I had made myself almost incapable of noticing the signals that the world around me was changing. The restaurants did not fail because of bad luck or the economy or even the competition. They failed because I was so busy defending the story I was telling myself about who I was and how things worked that I could no longer see what was actually happening.

Every piece of information that challenged my model was quietly filtered out. Every warning sign was explained away. Every person who tried to tell me that something fundamental was shifting was dismissed as someone who simply did not understand my vision. I was very good at protecting my sense of certainty, and that certainty was, without me realising it, destroying everything I had built.

What followed was not a neat or comfortable reinvention. It was a long, disorientating, and deeply human unravelling that took me into places I never expected to go, into therapy rooms, meditation retreats, and long stretches of uncomfortable self-inquiry, and eventually into the study of neuroscience, consciousness, and the strange ways in which human beings hold themselves inside familiar patterns even when those patterns are no longer serving them. I was not looking for business insights at the time. I was trying to understand how an intelligent, capable, hardworking person could miss something that, in hindsight, felt so obvious.

What I discovered in that process changed not only how I rebuilt my own life but how I now understand leadership, organisations, and change itself. I came to see that adaptability is not, at its core, a strategic capability. It is an emotional one. Our capacity to lead through uncertainty is directly limited by our capacity to stay regulated in our own nervous systems when we do not know what is coming next. Until we understand this, and until we treat adaptability as the human skill it actually is, our strategies, our transformation programmes, and our technological investments will continue to promise far more than they can deliver.

This is, in many ways, the book I wish someone had handed me before I lost everything.

To understand why, it helps to place the moment we are living through into a slightly longer historical perspective. Human progress has always moved in great waves, each one reshaping not only how we work but how we understand ourselves. The agricultural era was, at its heart, the age of muscle. For thousands of years, value was created primarily through physical labour, endurance, and the ability to work the land and build with one's hands. Then came the industrial era, which gradually became the age of the brain, where education, analysis, optimisation, and intellectual capability became the dominant currencies of success.

We are now entering another such transition, one that is being accelerated by artificial intelligence, and just as machines once made human muscle largely irrelevant as a source of value, they are now beginning to do the same thing to much of human cognition. This does not make human beings less important. It simply shifts the centre of gravity again, towards qualities that are harder to automate and far more difficult to cultivate, such as awareness, emotional intelligence, nervous system regulation, intuition, creativity, wisdom, and the quality of presence we bring into complex situations.

In other words, we are being invited into a different way of being human.

This is why this book is not really about technology, even though technology is part of the story, and it is not really about strategy, even though strategy matters. It is about the inner and outer work of evolution; about how leaders and organisations can learn to let go of identities, assumptions, and operating systems that once created success but now quietly limit what is possible; and about how to build the capacity to move with a world that is no longer predictable, stable, or easily controlled.

Over the pages that follow, we will explore why intelligent people so often stay stuck, why success can become a prison, and why organisations frequently defend the very things that are slowly making them irrelevant. We will look inside the neuroscience of adaptation, into how the brain and nervous system respond to uncertainty and threat, and then we will move outward into the practical architecture of adaptive organisations, into ideas like Today and Tomorrow Teams, the AI Strategy Scanner, and how to design for learning and evolution rather than for scale and efficiency alone.

But beneath all of this sits a much simpler and much more personal question, one that no framework can answer for you.

Are you willing to evolve?

Not as a role. Not as a job title. Not as a strategy.

As a human being.

Introduction

At the beginning of this book, I want to invite you into something practical, not just another idea to agree with, but a real reflection of where you stand today.

Most of us believe we are adaptable. We tell ourselves we are flexible, open-minded, even spontaneous. But neuroscience shows us something far more confronting, our brains are wired for familiarity, pattern, and certainty. What we often call adaptability is usually just comfort disguised as change.

That is why I created the Adaptability Quotient Assessment, a tool designed to help you and your organisation take an honest look at how adaptable you truly are. It is a way to measure your current mindset, your patterns, and your capacity to evolve in a world that refuses to stand still.

I encourage you to complete this assessment before moving through the book. Then return to it halfway through, and again at the end. The goal is not perfection, but awareness. Because you cannot transform what you have not first been willing to see.

This book is about building your Adaptive Intelligence™, and that begins with honesty.

Take the assessment here:

1 The Speed Mismatch

The world is moving faster than we are, and most of us haven't fully grasped what that means.

I learnt this the hardest way possible when my restaurant business collapsed. Not because we weren't working hard enough. Not because we didn't care about our customers. Not because we made obviously stupid decisions. But because the world had changed underneath us, and we hadn't changed with it.

We'd been successful for years. We had multiple locations, loyal customers, strong operations, and a clear identity in the market. We were doing everything that had always worked: refining our recipes, improving our service, optimising our costs, investing in our people. We were good at what we did. Really good.

But the market was shifting in ways we didn't see. Customer expectations were evolving. Technology was changing how people discovered and chose restaurants. New competitors were playing by different rules, offering different value propositions. The entire landscape was being reshaped.

And us? We kept optimising what we'd always done, making incremental improvements to a model that was quietly becoming obsolete.

By the time I realised the game had fundamentally changed, it was too late. The business failed. I had invested everything into building something meaningful and lost it all. I lost everything I'd worked for. Everything I thought I'd built.

That failure was devastating. But it was also the beginning of the most important learning of my life. Because in trying to understand what had actually happened, not just to my business but to my ability to see and respond to reality, I discovered something that applies far beyond restaurants. Something that's affecting every industry, every organisation, every leader trying to navigate today's world.

We're living through a period of exponential change, but our brains, our organisations, and our strategies are all built for linear change. And that mismatch is creating a crisis of adaptability across the entire business landscape.

The Exponential Reality We're Not Prepared For

Let me show you what we're actually dealing with, because most discussions of change miss the fundamental nature of what's happening.

For most of human history, change happened slowly enough that you could learn a set of skills, apply them throughout your career, and pass them on to the next generation with confidence they'd still be relevant. The world your parents knew looked roughly like the world you would know. Industries were stable enough to build 40-year careers. Competitive advantages lasted decades. Strategic planning horizons of 5 or 10 years made sense.

That world is gone.

Technology is advancing exponentially, not linearly. What this means in practice is that the amount of change we're experiencing in a single decade now exceeds what previous generations experienced in a lifetime.

Consider this: the first iPhone launched in 2007. Within five years, smartphones had transformed how we communicate, work, shop, navigate, consume media, and interact with the world. Entire industries were reshaped. Hundreds of thousands of jobs disappeared. Billions of dollars of value shifted from old players to new ones.

That's not linear change. That's exponential disruption compressed into a timeframe shorter than a typical product development cycle.

Or look at artificial intelligence. For decades, AI was mostly theoretical. Then, in the span of 18 months, we went from GPT-3 being a curiosity to AI fundamentally reshaping how knowledge work gets done. Tools that seemed impossible in 2022 were commonplace by 2024.

This is the new normal. Not occasional disruptions punctuating long periods of stability, but continuous, accelerating transformation across every domain.

And here's the critical insight: whilst technology advances exponentially, human organisations adapt linearly at best. Our decision-making processes, our organisational structures, our planning horizons, our mental models – they all evolved for a world where you could see change coming and have time to prepare for it.

This creates what I call the Speed Mismatch: the growing gap between how fast the external world is changing and how fast we can adapt our internal capabilities, structures, and strategies to match.

That gap isn't staying constant. It's widening every year. And for most organisations, it's becoming the defining strategic challenge of our era.

Why Traditional Planning Has Become Dangerous

I have spent years working with large organisations and governments on strategy and transformation, and I see the same patterns repeated across industries, from financial services to manufacturing to retail.

Companies would invest enormous resources into strategic planning. They'd hire expensive consultants. They'd conduct comprehensive market analysis. They'd run workshops with hundreds of senior leaders. They'd produce detailed five-year plans with clear initiatives, specific milestones, and measurable KPIs.

Then something would change in the market. A new technology, a regulatory shift, a competitor move, a change in customer behaviour. And those carefully crafted plans would become obsolete before the first initiative was even fully implemented.

The response was usually to plan better. More analysis. More scenarios. More contingencies. Better execution, but that wasn't the problem.

The problem was the fundamental assumption underlying traditional strategic planning: that the environment is stable enough to predict and prepare for. That assumption no longer holds.

Let me give you a concrete example from a manufacturing company I worked with recently. They'd spent 18 months developing what they believed was a comprehensive digital transformation strategy. They'd hired a top-tier consulting firm. They'd benchmarked best practices. They'd created detailed roadmaps covering technology infrastructure, process redesign, capability building, and change management.

The strategy document was 232 pages long. It was thorough, rigorous, well-researched. The CEO was proud of it. The board approved it. They were ready to execute.

By the time they actually began implementation, just six months after the strategy was finalised, three things had happened. First, their two main competitors had already implemented similar capabilities and moved on to the next wave of innovation. Second, the technology landscape had shifted enough that some of their chosen platforms were no longer the obvious choices. Third, customer expectations had evolved beyond what they'd planned for.

Their strategy wasn't wrong when they created it. It was just obsolete by the time they could execute it. The world had moved faster than their planning cycle.

This isn't about poor planning or lack of intelligence. This is about operating with a linear planning mindset in an exponential reality. It's like trying to navigate rapids by drawing a detailed map before you get in the water. By the time you've finished the map, the river has changed.

The Optimisation Trap

Here's where this gets psychologically interesting and where most organisations get trapped.

For decades, the playbook for business success was straightforward: find what works, optimise it, scale it, defend it. Build competitive advantages through efficiency, quality, and scale. Create moats that protect your position. This playbook worked brilliantly in stable environments.

But it's increasingly dangerous in volatile ones.

Why? Because the very things that create competitive advantage in stable environments – efficiency, optimisation, standardisation, specialisation – actively reduce your ability to adapt when the environment shifts.

When you optimise a system, you remove redundancy. You create tight coupling between components. You specialise capabilities. You make everything incredibly efficient for current conditions. This is brilliant when conditions stay roughly the same. It becomes catastrophic when conditions change fundamentally.

I lived this in my restaurant business. Over years of operation, we'd optimised everything. Our menu was refined to dishes we could execute consistently with maximum margin and taste. Our supply chain was streamlined to specific vendors offering the best prices and products. Our processes were standardised across locations. Our staff were trained in specific procedures. Our locations were chosen for demographics that matched our positioning.

We were incredibly efficient at delivering exactly what we'd always delivered, our operations were smooth, our costs were controlled, and our quality was consistent.

But that efficiency came at the cost of flexibility. When the market shifted, when customer preferences evolved, when new competitors emerged with different models, when technology changed the game, we couldn't adapt quickly.

Our menu optimisation meant we'd lost the capability to experiment with new concepts. Our supply chain efficiency meant we were locked into specific vendors and couldn't pivot quickly. Our process standardisation meant innovation felt like disruption. Our training made us excellent at the old game and unprepared for the new one.

We'd built a machine that was perfect for one environment and incapable of operating in another.

This is the optimisation trap, and it's not unique to restaurants; I see it everywhere. The manufacturing company so optimised for current production that they can't retool for new products, the bank so standardised in their processes that they can't accommodate new business models, and the retailer so efficient in their supply chain that they can't experiment with new fulfilment approaches.

Success breeds optimisation. Optimisation breeds rigidity. Rigidity breeds vulnerability.

Economies of Scale vs. Economies of Learning

Later in this book, I'm going to show you what becomes possible when you build an organisation around adaptability from the start rather than retrofitting it onto an existing structure.

I'll introduce you to Shein, the Chinese fashion company that has fundamentally disrupted the global apparel industry. Whilst traditional fast-fashion leaders like Zara built empires on economies of scale, producing large batches of garments and hoping they sell, Shein built something entirely different. They operate on what is called *economies of learning*.

Shein releases between 2,000 and 10,000 new styles every single day. Not every week. Every day. They produce tiny batches, measure real-time customer response, and scale production only on what customers actually want. Their supply chain isn't optimised for cost per unit – it's optimised for speed of learning.

The result? They've overtaken Zara and become the world's largest fashion retailer by doing the opposite of what traditional business wisdom would suggest. They've made their competitive advantage not efficiency but adaptability.

The Shein example illustrates something crucial about the Speed Mismatch: the companies that will thrive aren't those that plan better or optimise harder. They're the ones that build structures and cultures capable of continuous learning and rapid response. They're playing a different game entirely.

We'll explore this in depth when we look at Today and Tomorrow Teams and when I introduce you to the AI Strategy Scanner. But for now, understand this: the rules have changed, and most organisations are still playing by the old ones.

The Competence Trap

There's another psychological dimension to this that makes adaptation even harder: the better you are at what you do, the harder it becomes to do something different.

Your expertise becomes your prison. Your success becomes your blindness. Your strengths become your weaknesses.

I call this the Adaptation Paradox, and it operates at both individual and organisational levels.

At the individual level, experts develop deep pattern recognition in their domain. This allows them to make fast, accurate decisions within familiar contexts. But it also creates blind spots. They see new situations through the lens of past patterns. They dismiss anomalies that don't fit their mental models. They're so good at the current game that they can't see that the game itself is changing.

I watched this happen in my own thinking with the restaurants. I'd developed strong intuitions about what worked. When I'd see something new in the market, I'd automatically pattern match it to things I'd seen before. 'That's just a fad'. 'That won't work at scale'. 'Our customers don't want that'.

My expertise was actually preventing me from seeing reality clearly. I was so good at the old game that I couldn't recognise a new game was emerging. Successful companies develop strong cultures, clear identities, proven business models. These create alignment and efficiency, but they also create immune system responses to anything that threatens the current model.

I worked with a telecommunications company recently that was being disrupted by new technologies and business models. Their executive team intellectually understood they needed to change. They could articulate the threats; they'd studied the challengers. But organisationally, they couldn't adapt. Every new initiative that challenged the current model got rejected, not through explicit decisions but through a thousand small organisational antibodies. 'That's not how we do things here'. 'That won't work with our systems'. 'Our customers aren't ready for that'. 'That doesn't fit our brand'.

The very culture and capabilities that had made them successful were now preventing them from adapting to changed circumstances.

This is the competence trap: the capabilities that made you successful in one environment often prevent you from adapting to the next one.

What's Really Happening When We Fail to Adapt

After my restaurants failed, I became somewhat obsessed with understanding adaptation. Not just theoretically, but at a deep level. I read neuroscience, I studied psychology, I worked with dozens of companies across industries, I went on meditation retreats, and I did ayahuasca ceremonies in Peru.

I needed to understand not just what happened to my business but why I'd been so blind to the changes happening around me.

Why had I kept doubling down on approaches that weren't working? Why had I dismissed signals that, in retrospect, were obvious? Why had I felt such resistance to ideas that threatened my existing model?

What I discovered surprised me and changed everything I thought I knew about adaptation.

The barriers to adaptation aren't primarily about skills or knowledge or even strategy. They're about consciousness and emotional state. Let me explain what I mean by that, because this is crucial and most business thinking misses it entirely.

When we fail to adapt, it's usually not because we lack information. In most cases, the signals are there, the data exists, the trends are visible and the warnings are being sounded. We fail to adapt because we can't see or won't see what's actually happening. And that inability to see isn't about intelligence or analysis – it's about our psychological state.

During an ayahuasca ceremony in Peru (I know this might sound unusual, but stay with me because this is relevant to every leader reading this), I was shown, with brutal clarity, how my own unhealed trauma was creating blind spots in my perception.

I saw how my fear of failure made me defensive when people questioned my approach. How my need for control made me rigid in my thinking. How my identity as 'someone who built a successful business' made me unable to admit when that business model was failing. How my unresolved issues from my past were playing out in my business decisions in ways I couldn't see. My restaurant business hadn't failed because I lacked a good strategy or didn't work hard enough. It had failed because I was operating from a triggered, defensive psychological state that prevented me from seeing and responding to reality clearly.

And here's what I've discovered working with leaders and organisations: this is almost always what's happening when adaptation fails.

The CEO who can't pivot because their identity is too wrapped up in the current strategy. The executive team that rejects new ideas because they feel threatened by change. The organisation that clings to the old model because uncertainty feels more dangerous than continuing down a failing path.

These aren't rational decisions. They're emotional reactions driven by fear, trauma, and defensive patterns that operate below conscious awareness.

The Neuroscience of Stuck

There's solid neuroscience behind this, and understanding it is crucial for building genuine adaptive capacity. When we feel threatened and fundamental change is almost always experienced as threat, our brains shift into what neuroscientists call a *high beta state*. This is characterised by heightened activity in the amygdala, reduced activity in the prefrontal cortex, and a cascade of stress hormones.

In this state, we become more reactive and less reflective. Our thinking becomes narrower and more rigid. We focus on immediate threats rather than longer-term possibilities. We grasp for certainty even when certainty isn't available, and we defend our current position rather than exploring new options.

This is exactly what you don't want when you need to adapt to fundamental change. But it's exactly what happens for most people and organisations when confronted with such change.

I noticed this pattern in myself after my business failed; whenever someone would suggest a new approach, I'd feel my body tense. My mind would immediately start generating reasons why it wouldn't work, and I'd feel defensive, resistant, closed off. I was in a chronically triggered state. And in that state, I literally couldn't see possibilities. My perception was narrowed. My thinking was rigid. My emotional reactions were running the show, not my conscious decision-making.

The only way out of that state was to do the inner work: meditation, therapy, somatic practices, eventually plant medicine. I had to heal the trauma and fear that were keeping me stuck in defensive patterns.

This is true for organisations too. When a company is in a chronically threatened state, when the culture is defensive, when leadership is reactive, when people are operating from fear rather than possibility, adaptation becomes nearly impossible no matter how good your strategy is.

You cannot adapt effectively from a triggered state. You cannot see clearly when you're defensive. You cannot respond intelligently to change when you're driven by fear.

This is why the inner game matters as much as the outer game. Maybe more.

What Genuine Adaptability Actually Requires

So, if traditional planning doesn't work and if optimisation creates vulnerability and if our own psychology traps us in stuck patterns, what does work?

After years of studying this and working with organisations across industries, I've concluded that genuine adaptability requires three things, all of which are harder than most business books acknowledge.

First, you need to elevate awareness. Not in some vague, spiritual sense, but in a very practical way. You need to develop the ability to observe yourself and your organisation without defensive reactivity. To notice patterns without being trapped by them. To hold multiple perspectives simultaneously and to feel the discomfort of uncertainty without reflexively grasping for false certainty.

This is fundamentally about your level of consciousness and your emotional state, not just your analytical capabilities.

Second, you need to separate today from tomorrow at a structural level. Most organisations try to do both execution and exploration with the same people, same structures, same metrics, same incentives. This doesn't work. You need explicitly different teams with different mandates, different locations, different measures of success.

Today Teams run your current business brilliantly. Tomorrow Teams explore what could make that business obsolete. They're not the same people doing both. They're fundamentally different orientations requiring different capabilities.

Third, you need to simplify ruthlessly. Most strategies are too complex to actually guide decisions. Most structures have too many layers to respond quickly. Most processes have too many steps to iterate effectively.

Adaptability requires clarity and simplicity that enables fast decision-making without constant escalation and coordination.

These three elements – elevated awareness, today and tomorrow separation, ruthless simplification – form the core of genuine adaptive capacity. And we're going to explore each in depth in the chapters ahead.

What This Book Will Give You

This book is structured deliberately, because real adaptability is not a single shift, it is a layered process that unfolds across how you see the world, how you experience yourself, and how you design the systems you operate within. It moves from awareness to inner rewiring, to structural change, and finally to a personal decision about who you are willing to become in a world that is already moving.

First we unpack the real challenge beneath the surface. We explore the speed mismatch between an exponential world and linear thinking, why success quietly becomes a liability, and how identity, past patterns, and familiar ways of operating distort our ability to see clearly. Before anything can change, you need to understand why intelligent people and successful organisations still get stuck and what you are actually up against.

Then we move on to the inner game, because adaptation does not begin with strategy; it begins with state. You will understand the neuroscience behind how your brain responds to pressure, why survival mode blocks adaptive thinking, and why unprocessed experiences quietly shape your decisions, your leadership, and your organisation. This is where you learn that healing is not separate from performance, it is the foundation that determines whether any change will actually hold.

Then we focus on the outer game, where awareness becomes action. You will explore how organisations must be redesigned for continuous evolution, not periodic transformation, how to separate Today and Tomorrow work so efficiency does not kill adaptability, and how to simplify strategy so it creates movement rather than overwhelm. This is where adaptability becomes operational, structured, and real.

Finally, we step into a different way of operating. To recognise that this shift is not just technological or strategic, but deeply human, and that the future will favour those who can evolve their awareness, regulate their inner state, and lead from a place that matches the complexity of the world we are entering.

What you need to understand before we go further is this: this is not a book about incremental improvement or becoming slightly better at what already works. It is about a fundamental shift in how you perceive, decide, and operate, both personally and organisationally, in a world where the old rules are no longer stable.

That shift is more demanding than most frameworks admit. It asks you to confront the invisible patterns that have shaped your success, to loosen your attachment to identities that once served you, and to build new capabilities while actively unlearning the ones that no longer fit. At times, it will feel less like strategy and more like letting go, and less like learning and more like becoming.

But it is also the only approach that consistently works. Not just for surviving change, but for positioning yourself and your organisation to grow stronger because of it, to move with uncertainty rather than resist it, and to lead in a way that is aligned with the world that is already unfolding around you.

The Honest Promise

Let me be direct about what this book offers and what it doesn't, because I want to respect your intelligence and your time.

What it doesn't offer: a simple framework you can implement in 90 days. A five-step process that guarantees results.

A paint by numbers approach to transformation. Those things don't exist, despite what other business books might promise.

Real adaptation is messy, nonlinear, and deeply personal. It requires genuine inner work, not just strategic thinking. It demands uncomfortable changes, not just new processes.

What this book does offer: a comprehensive framework for building genuine adaptive capacity. Practical structures like Today and Tomorrow Teams that actually work. Tools like the AI Strategy Scanner that bring clarity to complex decisions. Most importantly, a clear-eyed understanding of why adaptation is hard and what actually needs to change.

The companies I've worked with that have implemented these frameworks have genuinely transformed their ability to sense and respond to change. But they've done so by doing the hard work, not by looking for shortcuts. By confronting their patterns, not by adding new initiatives on top of old structures. By healing their organisational trauma, not by denying it exists.

The leaders who've embraced this approach have become more conscious, more effective, and less reactive. But they've done so by facing their own psychological patterns and doing the inner work to evolve beyond them, not by learning new management techniques to deploy. This is work – real work, inner and outer. Personal and organisational. Strategic and psychological.

The question is, are you ready for it? Because here's what I know after my own journey and after working with hundreds of leaders: the Speed Mismatch isn't going away. The gap between external change and internal adaptation will keep widening, the pace will keep accelerating, and the pressure this creates will only become more intense for individuals and organisations alike.

The companies and leaders who thrive in the coming years will be those who build genuine adaptive capacity, the ability to sense change early, to respond without defensive reactivity, and to evolve continuously rather than waiting for crisis to force transformation. The world won't slow down for you, traditional playbooks won't save you, and incremental improvement won't be enough. In fact, optimisation will increasingly create vulnerability, and expertise will increasingly create blindness, not because these things are bad, but because they belong to a world that no longer exists.

What this means is that you need to fundamentally transform how you operate, how you think, how you lead, how you structure your organisation, how you make decisions, and even how you hold uncertainty itself. And that transformation does not begin with tools, strategies, or frameworks. It begins by understanding why you're stuck in the first place, why smart people, people like you, people like me, miss obvious signals and cling to failing approaches, why success itself quietly creates the conditions for future failure, and why our own psychology so often becomes the barrier to seeing and responding to reality.

That is what we need to explore next.

2

Why Smart People Stay Stuck

There is a particular kind of blindness that comes with success, and it is one of the most dangerous traps in business, not because it comes from stupidity or lack of intelligence but because it comes from having been right for a period of time and from having built an identity around the decisions that once worked. You can see this very clearly in what happened at Peloton.

At its peak, Peloton was not just a fitness company; it was a cultural phenomenon. It sat at the intersection of hardware, software, content, and community, and for a moment it looked like the future of fitness itself. Demand exploded, the share price soared, and the company became the symbol of a world that had moved indoors, where premium connected experiences were not a luxury but a new normal.

And that success was not an accident. Peloton's leadership team was smart, ambitious, and genuinely visionary. They had created something new and compelling, and for a while, the world rewarded them for it. But as the pandemic ended and the world began to open up again, the underlying conditions that had fuelled that explosive growth started to change. Gyms reopened. Consumer behaviour shifted. Demand softened. The obvious move was to slow down, cut costs, and reframe the business for a different kind of future.

Instead, Peloton kept building as if the old world was still in place. They doubled down on manufacturing, overexpanded their footprint, and held on to the story that the surge was not an anomaly but a permanent shift. From the outside, this looked like bad forecasting or operational missteps. In reality, it was something much deeper.

Peloton's identity had become entangled with the version of the world in which it had won. Letting go of that story would have meant admitting that the conditions that made them great were temporary and that the business now needed to become something different.

And this is the part that matters: Peloton did not struggle because its leaders were incapable or unintelligent. They struggled because their success made it emotionally difficult to see clearly. Their intelligence did not save them; it gave them better reasons to believe they could extend a past that was already ending.

This is what I want you to understand. The barriers to adaptation are almost never about capability. They are about identity, emotion, and the invisible psychological commitments that make it hard to see reality when reality no longer matches the story you have been telling yourself.

The Success Trap

Let me start with a paradox that sits at the heart of why adaptation is so difficult: the very things that make you successful in one context often become the barriers to success in the next context.

This isn't just about expertise, though that's part of it. It's about something deeper and more insidious.

When you succeed at something, you naturally develop strong beliefs about what works. These beliefs get encoded not just in your conscious thinking but in your automatic patterns, your instincts, your identity. They become part of who you are, not just what you know.

I experienced this acutely with my restaurant business. We'd built something successful using specific approaches. We had beliefs about what customers wanted, how restaurants should operate, what made for good service, how to price, where to locate, what to offer.

These beliefs had been validated by years of success. They'd been reinforced thousands of times through positive results and genuinely felt like the truth, not opinion.

When the market started shifting, these deeply held beliefs became my blindness. I couldn't see the changes clearly because my perception was filtered through beliefs that were no longer accurate. Every signal that contradicted my beliefs got dismissed or rationalised away. Every idea that challenged my approach felt wrong, even dangerous.

It wasn't that I was stupid or stubborn, though from the outside it might have looked that way. It's that my success had created deep neural pathways, automatic ways of seeing and responding that operated below conscious awareness.

This is what makes the success trap so vicious. The more successful you've been with a particular approach, the stronger those neural pathways become, the harder it is to see or do anything different. Your success literally rewires your brain in ways that reduce your adaptability.

The German Car Industry: A Masterclass in Getting Stuck

I want to share an example that illustrates this dynamic at an industry level, because it shows how even the most capable, most intelligent, most resourced organisations can fall into the success trap.

For decades, German automotive engineering was synonymous with excellence. Mercedes, BMW, Volkswagen, Audi,

Porsche. . .these weren't just car companies. They were symbols of precision engineering, quality craftsmanship, and technical superiority. The combustion engine, refined over a century, had reached extraordinary levels of sophistication in German hands. Hundreds of precisely machined parts working in perfect harmony. Power, efficiency, and reliability that competitors struggled to match.

German car manufacturers invested billions into their combustion engine capabilities. They built vast factory complexes designed specifically for assembling engines with hundreds of components. They trained generations of engineers in the art of internal combustion. They developed supply chains spanning continents, all optimised for a particular way of building cars.

And they were spectacularly successful. German cars commanded premium prices worldwide. They defined what excellence looked like in the automotive industry.

Then, about a decade ago, something shifted. China began investing heavily in battery technology and electric vehicle supply chains. Not because China was better at combustion engines (they weren't) but precisely because they weren't trapped by success in the old paradigm. They had nothing to lose by betting on a different future.

What did the German manufacturers do? They doubled down on what they knew. They made their combustion engines even more refined. They added more features, more power, more efficiency. They were so good at what they'd always done that they couldn't imagine a world where it wouldn't matter.

Meanwhile, electric vehicles don't need engines with hundreds of precision parts. They need batteries, electric motors, and software. The entire manufacturing paradigm is different. Simpler assembly. Fewer components. Different supply chains. Different skills.

Today, the German car industry is facing an existential crisis. Chinese electric vehicles are increasingly seen as superior, not just cheaper but better, faster, simpler to build, and more aligned with where the market is heading. The very excellence that defined German automotive engineering has become a liability.

And here's what I want you to understand: this isn't about intelligence. German automotive engineers are among the best in the world. It isn't about resources. These companies had billions to invest. It isn't about information – the trends were visible for years.

It's about the success trap. When you've built your entire identity, your organisational structure, your supply chains, your skills, your reputation around one way of doing things, it becomes almost impossible to see or embrace a fundamentally different way, even when the evidence is overwhelming.

The German car industry didn't fail to adapt because they lacked the capability to build electric vehicles. They failed to adapt because their success in the old paradigm created massive psychological, structural, and financial barriers to embracing the new one.

This is why I keep emphasising that adaptability isn't primarily an intellectual or strategic challenge. It's an emotional and structural one. The German car executives could see the data. They could analyse the trends. But they couldn't let go of who they'd been long enough to become who they needed to be.

The Sunk Cost of Identity

There is another psychological dynamic at play here that is even more powerful than outdated beliefs, and that is our investment in identity. Every leader and every organisation have invested enormously in becoming who they currently are, through years of effort, sacrifice, resource allocation, reputation building, and the slow construction of a self-concept that says, 'This is who we are and this is what we do'. Over time, that identity does not just describe reality; it becomes the lens through which reality is interpreted and defended.

When the world shifts and that identity is no longer optimal, we are not just facing a strategic or operational challenge; we are facing something far more intimate and far more difficult. Adapting is not only about learning new skills or adopting new strategies but also about letting go of who we have been, and that feels like loss – and in many cases like a kind of psychological death. The deeper and more successful the identity, the more threatening that letting go becomes.

You can see this very clearly in what happened at Peloton. For a period of time, Peloton was not simply a fitness company; it was a symbol of a new way of living, a premium, connected, at-home experience that felt inevitable and permanent. The company's identity, its culture, and its internal narratives became built around the idea that it was not just riding a temporary wave but reshaping an entire industry. When the world began to reopen and behaviour started to shift back towards gyms and outdoor life, the challenge was not merely to adjust forecasts or reduce costs; it was to accept that the story they had built about who they were and what the future looked like was no longer true in the same way.

If the surge in demand was situational rather than structural, what did that say about the company's self-image? If the world did not stay indoors, what did that mean for the version of the future they had committed themselves to? And if the business now needed to become leaner, more cautious, and more operationally disciplined, who were they, really, if not the category-defining hypergrowth story they had come to believe in?

These are not just ego questions, although ego is certainly involved. They are much deeper questions about meaning, worth, and identity, and until they are addressed at that level, no amount of strategic analysis or financial modelling will produce real change. This is what I mean by the sunk cost of identity. We have invested so much in becoming who we are that changing who we are starts to feel impossibly expensive, and so we keep doubling down on approaches that no longer fit, not because we do not know better but because the psychological cost of change feels higher than the cost of staying the same.

You can see the same pattern at an even larger scale in the German automotive industry, where manufacturers did not just invest money in being the best combustion-engine builders in the world; they invested identity. Entire engineering cultures, career paths, organisational pride, and even national self-image were wrapped up in a particular kind of excellence. Walking away from that was never just a technical or economic decision. It felt, at a very real level, like walking away from themselves.

When Expertise Becomes Prison

Let me go deeper into the expertise paradox I mentioned in the first chapter, because this is crucial for understanding why smart people stay stuck, and why it is, as the saying goes, so difficult to see the label of the bottle from inside the bottle once your way of seeing the world has quietly become the world itself.

Expertise is pattern recognition that has been deeply encoded through repetition and reward, and when an expert sees a situation, they do not consciously analyse it piece by piece; they see the whole pattern instantly and know the appropriate response, without effort, without friction, without even noticing that a judgement has been made.

This is what makes experts so effective in stable domains. A chess master sees patterns on the board that novices cannot perceive. An experienced doctor recognises symptom patterns instantly. A seasoned executive senses organisational dynamics others miss.

But here is the trap, and it is subtle: experts do not just see patterns; they see patterns they have seen before, and when confronted with something genuinely new, something that does not fit their existing models, they unconsciously try to force it into familiar categories rather than staying present with what is actually in front of them, which is why we do not know who discovered water, but we do know it was not a fish.

I watched this play out with a retail executive I worked with. She had spent 30 years in traditional retail, rising through the ranks at major chains, and she was exceptional at store operations, merchandising, inventory management – all the skills that had made retail successful for decades and had earned her every promotion she had received. When her company needed to develop e-commerce capabilities, she could not see it clearly, because every conversation about online shopping was filtered through her store-based mental models. 'How do we create the in-store experience online?' 'What's the digital equivalent of our floor layout?' 'How do we translate our merchandising approach?'

These were not irrational questions, but they were the wrong questions, because they were trying to make the new world fit the old patterns rather than recognising that e-commerce required fundamentally different thinking. Her expertise, her hard-won knowledge about retail, had become a cognitive prison. She literally could not see the new game, because her brain was automatically pattern-matching it to the old one.

This is why bringing in outsiders can be so valuable, not because they are smarter or more capable but because they do not suffer from the expert's blindness, and they can often see what is actually there rather than what merely fits the patterns they already know.

The Comfort of Certainty

There's another psychological factor that keeps intelligent people stuck, and that's our deep need for certainty. Human brains are prediction machines; we're constantly trying to predict what will happen next so we can prepare appropriate responses. Uncertainty is neurologically uncomfortable. It activates threat responses. It feels dangerous.

When you're an expert, when you're successful, when you've mastered a domain, you have certainty. You know what to do. You know what works. You know how things will unfold. That certainty feels good. It feels safe. It feels like competence.

Adaptation requires giving up that certainty. It requires operating in ambiguity, not knowing if your new approach will work, feeling your way forward rather than executing from confident knowledge. For successful people who've built their careers on competence and certainty, this is deeply uncomfortable. So unconsciously, they avoid situations that require it. They stay in domains where they have certainty rather than venture into spaces where they don't.

I felt this acutely during my restaurant crisis, when people would suggest new approaches, new concepts, new ways of operating, part of me knew they might be right. But another part of me felt the terror of not knowing. If I abandoned what I knew, I'd be operating without a map, without certainty about what would work. That fear of uncertainty kept me paralysed far longer than logic would suggest. I kept trying to make the old approaches work, not because I thought they were optimal but because they were certain. I knew how to execute them even if they weren't succeeding.

The comfort of certainty, even false certainty, is powerful. It takes conscious effort and psychological work to become comfortable operating in genuine uncertainty.

The Emotional Cost of Being Wrong

Let's be honest about something that doesn't get discussed enough in business contexts: being wrong, especially about important things, is emotionally painful.

When you've been publicly confident about a strategy or approach, when you've convinced others to follow you, when you've staked your reputation on being right, discovering you were wrong isn't just an intellectual adjustment – it's a psychological blow.

The more senior you are, the more painful this becomes. CEOs, executives, senior leaders – they're not supposed to be wrong. They're supposed to be the people who see clearly, who make good decisions, who have the answers. Admitting they got something fundamental wrong threatens their entire position and identity.

So they don't. Or more accurately, they can't. Their brain won't let them see evidence that they're wrong because the emotional cost is too high. The psychological defences activate automatically, generating rationalisations, dismissing contrary evidence, finding reasons why the current approach just needs more time or better execution.

This isn't conscious dishonesty. It's how human psychology protects us from painful realisations. But it's also what keeps us stuck in failing approaches long after we should have changed course. I see this pattern constantly in organisations. The longer a leader has been committed to a particular strategy, the harder it becomes for them to see evidence that it's not working. They're psychologically invested in being right. Their brain actively filters out information that would prove them wrong.

The only way past this is developing what I call meta-awareness: the ability to observe your own psychological processes, to notice when you're defending rather than seeing clearly, to catch yourself rationalising rather than learning.

This is hard work. It requires genuine humility, emotional maturity, and often support from others who can help you see your blind spots.

Why Being Right Makes It Worse

Here's something counterintuitive: the smarter you are, the more capable you are of sophisticated self deception.

Intelligence is brilliant at generating rationalisations. When you're smart, you can construct elaborate, seemingly logical explanations for why your current approach is still valid despite contrary evidence. You can find patterns in noise. You can develop theories that explain away anomalies. You can make sophisticated arguments that convince yourself and others that you're not stuck, you're being appropriately cautious or strategic.

I've seen this with extremely intelligent leaders more times than I can count. They're not in denial in any simple sense. They've done analysis. They've considered alternatives. They've thought deeply about the situation. And precisely because of all that cognitive work, they're even more convinced they're right when they're actually caught in sophisticated rationalisation.

This is why external perspectives matter so much. Why coaches, advisors, board members who aren't wrapped up in your psychology can see things you can't. Not because they're smarter, but because they're not invested in your rationalisations.

The Accumulation of Small Choices

It's rarely one big wrong decision. It's an accumulation of small choices, each of which seems reasonable at the time, that collectively create a trajectory towards irrelevance.

Each individual decision to delay a pivot. Each choice to optimise the current model rather than experiment with new ones. Each time you prioritise short term results over long-term positioning. Each moment you dismiss a weak signal because it doesn't fit your mental model.

None of these decisions feels dangerous. Each one feels prudent, reasonable, maybe even necessary. But they compound over time, creating momentum in a direction that becomes increasingly difficult to change.

This is why adaptability requires active, conscious attention. The default trajectory of any successful organisation is towards increasing rigidity. Without deliberate effort to maintain flexibility, to question assumptions, to explore alternatives, you drift towards obsolescence through a thousand small, reasonable decisions.

The Courage to Explore Outside Your Domain

What the German car industry example teaches us, what my restaurant failure taught me, what I've seen in organisation after organisation, is that staying stuck isn't primarily about intelligence or resources or even strategy.

It's about the lack of courage to explore what's possible outside your current domain.

When you're excellent at something, when you've built your identity around that excellence, venturing outside feels terrifying. You go from expert to novice. From certain to uncertain. From competent to confused.

Most people and organisations avoid that discomfort by staying in their lane, by continuing to refine what they already know, by making the combustion engine even more perfect whilst the world moves to batteries.

This is why, later in this book, I'll introduce the concept of Today and Tomorrow Teams. The fundamental insight is that you cannot ask the same people who are excellent at today's business to simultaneously explore what might make that business obsolete. The psychological demands are too different – the identity threats are too real.

You need separate structures, separate people, separate locations, separate metrics for the work of exploring outside your current domain. Not because your Today people lack intelligence but because their very excellence creates barriers to seeing and embracing fundamentally different futures.

Breaking Free Requires More Than Strategy

Everything I've described in this chapter – the success trap, the sunk cost of identity, expertise as prison, the comfort of certainty, the emotional cost of being wrong, the organisational immune system – adds up to a crucial insight: you cannot think your way out of being stuck.

The barriers are not primarily intellectual. They're psychological, emotional, neurological. They operate below conscious awareness. They're encoded in your automatic patterns, your defensive reactions, your sense of self.

This is why most strategic planning processes fail to create real change. They're addressing the problem at the wrong level. They're trying to solve with analysis what can be solved only through transformation of consciousness and identity.

This isn't some soft, touchy feely addition to 'real' strategic work. This is the actual work. Without it, your strategies will keep getting undermined by psychological patterns you can't see.

The companies that successfully adapt aren't those with the best strategies, though strategy matters. They're the ones where leaders have done enough inner work to see clearly, to respond without defensive reactivity, to let go of what's no longer serving them even when it's painful.

That's what the next part of this book addresses. Not what you need to do, but who you need to become. Not what structures to implement, but what consciousness to develop. Not what plans to make, but what healing to undergo.

Because here's the truth: stuck isn't primarily a strategic problem. It's a psychological one. And solving it requires going deeper than most business books dare to go.

Let's go there together.

3 The Identity Trap

Who are you when everything you've built becomes obsolete?

This sounds like a philosophical question, but it isn't, not really, because it is one of the most practical and confronting questions any human being can face when the world around them changes faster than the story they have been telling about themselves. Strip it right back and you realise that the deepest barrier to adaptation is almost never a lack of skill or strategy or resources or even intelligence; it is the much quieter and more stubborn thing we call identity, the invisible structure that holds together who we believe we are, what we believe we deserve, and what kind of life feels normal to us.

Let me ask you something uncomfortable, and don't answer it too quickly. If the role you play in the world disappeared tomorrow, if the status, the title, the expertise, the thing you have spent years building suddenly stopped being relevant, who would you be then, and more importantly, what would you still be allowed to want? Most of us never really ask this, because we build our lives in such a way that we do not have to, and yet the world has a habit of asking it for us at the worst possible moments.

You can see this identity trap most clearly in the strange and tragic stories of people who win vast amounts of money in the lottery and somehow manage to lose it all again within a few years, not because they do not understand spreadsheets or budgets, although that is often part of it, but because their inner world is still organised around being someone who struggles, someone who complains that the system is against them, someone for whom life is hard and unfair and slightly hostile. That identity has been rehearsed for decades, and it comes with a whole set of stories, friendships, habits, and emotional rewards. When money suddenly arrives, it does not just change their bank balance; it threatens their entire sense of self. They no longer get to play the role they know how to play. In a strange way, they are no longer on the side they have always believed they were on, and so, often without realising it, they make decisions that take them right back to the only identity that feels like home.

The opposite pattern is just as revealing. When people who are deeply identified as builders, creators, or wealth generators lose everything, they often make it back far faster than logic or circumstance would suggest. Not because they are lucky, and not because they are working harder than everyone else, but because their identity has already organised their nervous system, their expectations, and their way of seeing the world around being someone who creates value at that level. Even when the external structure collapses, the internal one is still intact, and so they begin, almost automatically, to behave in ways that re-create the world they are used to living in.

This is why some people can work relentlessly for their entire lives and never seem to get ahead, while others appear to move with far less effort and somehow always end up in positions of leverage, opportunity, or wealth. It is not just about effort or talent or timing. It is about what feels normal, what feels allowed, and what kind of life your identity is quietly but relentlessly steering you back towards, again and again.

This is the real trap, and it shows up everywhere, in careers, in organisations, in relationships, and in entire industries. We do not resist change because we are stupid or lazy, we resist it because, at a deep level, change threatens the story of who we are, and most of us would rather defend a familiar identity, even a painful or limiting one, than step into a version of ourselves we do not yet know how to be.

And until you understand this, not as an idea but as something that is operating in you, quietly shaping what you reach for, what you avoid, and what you unconsciously return to, real adaptation will always feel strangely hard, even when, on paper, it makes perfect sense.

The Architecture of Identity

Identity isn't just a story you tell about yourself. It's the fundamental organising principle of your psychology. It determines what you pay attention to, what you value, what choices feel natural vs. what feels threatening or wrong. It operates largely below conscious awareness, shaping your perception and behaviour automatically.

When you say 'I am a lawyer' or 'I am an entrepreneur' or 'I am a leader in manufacturing', you're not just describing what you do. You're naming a complex structure of beliefs, values, behaviours, and social relationships that define how you see yourself and how you operate in the world.

That identity structure was built over years, probably decades. Every success reinforced it. Every social interaction within your professional community strengthened it. Every decision you made in accordance with it deepened the neural pathways. Your brain literally rewired itself around this identity.

And here's what makes adaptation so difficult: when circumstances change such that your identity is no longer optimal, your brain experiences this as existential threat. Not metaphorical threat. Actual neurological threat responses, the same systems that activate when you're in physical danger.

This is why people often become defensive, rigid, even irrational when their identity is challenged. It's not weakness or stubbornness. It's neurology. Their brain is doing exactly what it's designed to do: protect the self-structure from dissolution.

That fusion of identity and circumstance made it nearly impossible for me to see clearly or respond effectively in my business meltdown. I wasn't protecting a business strategy; I was protecting my sense of self.

Professional Identity as Prison

If there is one place where intelligent, capable people get quietly trapped, it is inside their professional identity, because over the years you do not just build skills and experience; you build a story about who you are in the world, what you are good for, where your value comes from, and how you justify your place in the room. You accumulate competence, recognition, status, and results, and all of that slowly crystallises into something that feels solid and reassuring, a sense of self that gives you confidence, social capital, and meaning, and a very clear answer to the question, 'What do you do?'

The problem is that this same identity, the one that has rewarded you so well, also quietly draws the edges of what you can see and what you are willing to become without feeling like you are betraying yourself. Think of the executive who has built an entire career on being the person who makes things run smoothly, who brings order, predictability, and control to complex systems, and notice what happens when their organisation suddenly needs to become more experimental, more comfortable with ambiguity, and more willing to fail in order to learn. At a rational level they may completely understand the argument, but at a deeper level it feels like being asked to step away from the very thing that made them valuable in the first place, and so their nervous system resists, not because they are stubborn or unintelligent but because their identity is being quietly threatened.

This is why you see the same pattern everywhere, the brilliant engineer who struggles when the role becomes more commercial, the relationship driven sales leader who resists a world of data and algorithms, the visionary founder who finds it excruciating when the company needs discipline more than inspiration. The cruel irony is that the very capabilities that built your professional identity are often the ones that later become the walls of the prison you did not realise you were constructing.

Organisational Identity Runs Even Deeper

What is true for individuals becomes even more powerful, and more constraining, when it shows up at the level of organisations, because companies do not just have strategies and structures; they have identities, shared stories about who they are that quietly shape how thousands of people think, decide, and act every day, often without anyone ever needing to say them out loud. 'We are about quality', 'we are about efficiency', 'we are about scale', or 'we are about design' are not just slogans; they are organising principles that create coherence, pride, and speed, allowing large groups of people to move in the same direction without constant coordination or instruction.

But the same identity that creates this coherence also draws invisible boundaries around what the organisation can become without feeling like it is betraying itself. I saw this beautifully illustrated in a short documentary about Ikea, a company whose entire operating model, from supply chains to engineering to culture, is built around precision, repeatability, and the ruthless elimination of imperfection in order to produce beautiful, functional objects at massive scale. At one point, their designers wanted to create a vase that looked slightly off, subtly bent, imperfect in a way that felt human and handmade, and what sounded like a simple creative idea turned into months of struggle, because their systems, their processes, and their way of thinking were all optimised to do the exact opposite, to produce straight lines, right angles, and identical outcomes every single time.

The problem was not technical capability, because they had some of the best engineers in the world, and it was not a lack of understanding, because everyone could see why the idea was appealing, but organisationally they were trying to do something that contradicted their deepest identity. They were asking a machine built for perfection to learn how to produce imperfection on purpose, and that turns out to be far harder than it sounds. In the end, once they fully realised how deeply this one 'imperfect' idea disrupted their processes, their thinking, and their entire way of working, they quietly abandoned it and went back to doing what they had always done best, creating objects that were perfectly balanced, perfectly aligned, and perfectly repeatable, not because the idea was bad but because it asked them to become something their identity simply could not sustain. No amount of planning or project management could have changed that, because the real challenge was never how to make the vase; it was how to step outside of who they had spent decades becoming.

The Sunk Cost of Becoming

There is a particular psychological dynamic that makes identity change so difficult, and I think of it as the sunk cost of becoming, because you have invested enormous resources into turning yourself into who you currently are, years of education and training, the sacrifice of other possible paths, financial investment, emotional energy, social capital, all of it patiently channelled into developing a particular identity and a particular way of moving through the world.

In economic terms, these are sunk costs, investments that cannot be recovered, and rationally they should not influence future decisions, because what matters is not what you have already spent but what will create value going forward. But humans are not rational about sunk costs, especially when those costs are not just financial but personal, psychological, and existential, because the more you have invested in becoming who you are, the more painful it feels to even consider letting that version of yourself go, even when it becomes increasingly clear that the world has changed or that the life you built no longer quite fits.

This is why I have always loved David Brooks' book *The Second Mountain* and why I think he is such a deep and honest thinker about what it means to build a life, because he describes how most of us spend our early years climbing a first mountain, building a career that made sense to our parents, choosing paths that earned approval, status, and security, creating lives that look successful from the outside, only to arrive at the top and quietly realise that this was never really our mountain in the first place.

The hardest part, as he describes it, is not admitting that the first mountain was the wrong one; it is having the courage to climb back down into the valley, to let go of the identity you worked so hard to construct, and to begin the slow, uncertain climb up a second mountain that is actually your own. And this is exactly what happens in organisations and careers when markets change or meaning shifts, because the sunk cost is not just time or money or effort; it is the person you have become, and writing that off, even when the alternative is stagnation or irrelevance, can feel psychologically more expensive than staying exactly where you are.

Status and Social Identity

Identity is never just an internal, private story we tell ourselves; it is deeply social, continuously shaped, reinforced, and stabilised by the groups we belong to and the communities that recognise and reward us for being who we are, which means that who you become is not only about your own preferences or talents but also about where you get approval, belonging, and status. Your identity is constantly being mirrored back to you by the people around you, and over time you begin to unconsciously organise your life, your behaviour, and even your ambitions around maintaining your place in those social systems.

This is why changing identity is never just about changing how you see yourself; it is also about changing your position inside hierarchies and social circles that matter to you, and that can be far more threatening than most people realise. We all do this in small, everyday ways. If you like to have a beer after work, you tend to find yourself surrounded by people who do the same, and before long your friendships, your routines, and even your sense of what counts as 'normal' start to orbit around that habit. If you smoke marijuana, your social world quietly reorganises itself around people who also smoke marijuana. If you are obsessed with Ironman competitions or endurance sports, your weekends, your conversations, and your friendships start filling up with people who share that same addiction to pushing their bodies to extremes. Our social circles are not just built around interests; they are built around identities, and very often around the substances, habits, and rituals we use to relax, cope, or feel like ourselves. I have never really been a drinker, and over the years I have noticed that I simply do not sustain close friendships with people for whom drinking is a central part of their social life, not because anyone is right or wrong, but because at the level of identity and lifestyle we are living in different worlds.

The same dynamic plays out, just in more formal clothing, in professional life. Think about an academic who has built their reputation inside a particular theoretical school, whose identity is not just 'professor' but 'leading scholar in this specific approach', and whose status is reinforced through invitations to conferences, editorial roles, citations, and recognition from others in that same intellectual tribe. If they were to shift to a different framework, even one that might be more relevant to the problems of the present, they would not just be changing their ideas; they would be voluntarily stepping down in status, losing social capital, and becoming a learner again in a community whose respect they deeply value.

This is why the social cost of identity change can be just as powerful, and sometimes more powerful, than the psychological or strategic one, because you are not only risking your own sense of competence, you are risking your belonging, your status, and your place in the tribe, and for a deeply social species like ours, that can feel like a much bigger threat than almost any business problem.

The Courage to Let Go

Everything I have described so far can start to sound a little bleak, because if identity is this powerful, this deeply encoded, and this socially reinforced, it is natural to ask how anyone ever manages to adapt to fundamental change at all. This is where we need to talk about something that is almost never discussed seriously in business or leadership contexts, and that is the courage to let go of who you have been in order to become who you need to be.

This is not courage in some abstract, heroic sense; it is a very specific psychological capacity, the ability to tolerate the discomfort of identity dissolution without either defending the old identity or prematurely grasping for a new one, and it sits at the heart of every real transformation, whether that transformation is personal, organisational, or civilisational. Because all transformations, without exception, move through the same three phases, whether you are changing jobs, moving countries, ending a relationship, or, as we are now, moving as a species from the industrial age into an age shaped by AI, quantum computing, and entirely new ways of understanding reality.

The first phase is always sadness, the quiet or sometimes not so quiet grief of leaving the shore of familiarity, of stepping away from comfort, certainty, and the identity you may have spent 10, 20, or 30 years carefully constructing. Even when the old world is clearly no longer working, even when you can see that change is necessary, there is still a real sense of loss in letting go of who you have been, because that identity has given you orientation, status, and a story about who you are in the world.

The second phase is what I think of as strange, arriving in a new land that does not yet make sense, a world you do not have the skills for, a landscape that keeps shifting under your feet so that every time you think you have learned the rules, the rules change again. This is the phase we are very much in right now, collectively, and it is the phase most people try to solve purely with their intellect, by reading more, planning more, analysing more, as if this were just a cognitive problem to be fixed. But the truth is that this is not primarily an intellectual transition, it is an emotional one, and until the emotional layer is processed, the mind will stay locked in anxiety, resistance, and anger.

C.S. Lewis captured this beautifully when he said, 'I sat with my anger long enough until she told me her name was grief', because what we so often experience as irritation, cynicism, or outrage about change is actually unprocessed sadness about what we are losing. If that grief is not felt and metabolised, we never really arrive in the new world; we only stand at its edge, resentful, fearful, and suspicious, interpreting everything through the lens of what has already disappeared.

The third phase of transformation is always adventure, the moment when the wind comes back into your sails, when the new terrain starts to make sense, when you begin to see a path forward and feel your own energy and curiosity return. But you cannot skip to that phase. You have to pass through sad and strange to get there, and right now, as individuals and as organisations, we are very much living in the long, uncomfortable space between the two.

This is why the courage to let go is not a slogan or a motivational idea, it is a real inner practice, because letting go has to happen before the new identity is clear. You have to be willing to exist in that in-between space, where the old story about who you are has started to dissolve, but the new one has not yet formed, and that space is deeply uncomfortable for the nervous system and for the mind. It feels like being unmoored, like not quite knowing who you are or where you belong, and most people will do almost anything to avoid staying there for long.

So either they cling to the old identity long after it has stopped serving them or they rush into a new one that is really just a rearranged version of the old, because it feels safer than not knowing. Real adaptation, however, requires being able to stay in that strange, uncertain middle, to let go of certainty about who you are, to allow the old self-structure to dissolve without panic, and to trust that something more fitting will emerge in its own time.

This is not strategic work, it is not about plans or frameworks or roadmaps, it is psychological and emotional work, and without it, no amount of clever thinking will ever produce genuine, lasting adaptability.

Beyond the Mask

There is something quietly liberating, and at first deeply uncomfortable, about realising that you cannot truly change your life by simply trying to swap one identity for a better one, because that whole approach still assumes that identity is something solid and defining, something you have to upgrade rather than question. As long as you are trying to move from one version of yourself to another, you are still living inside the same structure, just redecorating the same room, and often all you are really doing is trading one carefully constructed prison for another that looks more impressive on the outside. Real freedom begins when you start to see that identity itself is far more fluid and provisional than you were taught; that you can have roles, capabilities, and responsibilities without fusing your entire sense of self to them; that you can be a leader, or a builder, or a creator without any of those things becoming who you think you are at your core.

I did not come to understand this as a theory but through direct inner work, where there were moments of seeing with unsettling clarity that the story I called 'me' was not a solid thing at all, but a bundle of memories, narratives, and beliefs my mind had been holding together and treating as if it were fixed. At first that recognition is destabilising, because if you are not the story you have been telling about yourself, then the obvious question is who are you, but on the other side of that fear there is an unexpected lightness, because if you are not fundamentally any single identity, then you are free to meet life as it comes, to succeed without success defining you, to fail without failure collapsing you, and to adapt without adaptation feeling like a kind of self-betrayal. This is what it really means to change your relationship to identity, not by becoming someone else but by loosening your attachment to the whole idea that you need to be someone in the first place, and this is deep work, not strategic work, because it changes the structure that creates stuckness rather than just rearranging its surface.

What This Means for Leadership

If you're a leader reading this, you're probably thinking: this is fascinating, but what do I actually do with it? How does understanding identity traps translate into practical leadership in my organisation?

Here's what I've learned: the most important thing you can do is start with yourself. Not because you need to fix yourself before you can help others, but because you can't guide others through identity transformation if you haven't done at least some of that work yourself.

Start noticing how your own identity shapes your perception and decisions. When you resist an idea or approach, ask yourself: is this resistance based on clear strategic thinking, or is it because the idea threatens something about how I see myself?

When you feel defensive in a conversation, pause and notice: what's being threatened here? What aspect of my identity is feeling at risk?

When you find yourself clinging to an approach that's not working, get curious: what would I have to let go of about myself to try something different?

This isn't about judging yourself or trying to eliminate ego. It's about developing awareness of how identity operates in you. That awareness creates choice where before there was only automatic reaction.

For your organisation, the most important thing is creating psychological safety for identity work. People need to be able to question who they've been without feeling that they'll be punished or marginalised. They need support for the discomfort of identity transition, not pressure to skip past it quickly.

This might mean slowing down certain change processes to allow time for psychological adaptation. It might mean explicitly acknowledging what's being let go and creating rituals to honour it. It might mean bringing in support for people doing difficult identity work.

It definitely means being willing to have conversations at an emotional and psychological level, not just strategic and operational. Most leaders are uncomfortable with this. They want to stay in the safe territory of analysis and planning. But identity work happens in the emotional territory, and leaders need to be willing to go there.

The Integration Challenge

Here's something crucial: you can't skip from understanding that identity is constructed to being free of identity concerns. There's a necessary integration process.

In spiritual communities, there's sometimes a trap of using the recognition that 'identity is illusory' as a way to bypass the actual psychological work of identity transformation. People have genuine insights about the constructed nature of self and then try to operate as if they're beyond identity concerns when actually they're just suppressing them.

In business contexts, I see a parallel trap. Leaders recognise intellectually that identity is limiting adaptability and then try to will themselves beyond identity concerns through force of analysis or strategy – it doesn't work.

You have to honour the psychological reality of identity, even as you see through it conceptually. You have to work with your identity patterns, not try to transcend them through intellectual understanding alone. This means doing the actual inner work: meditation, therapy, somatic practices, whatever helps you develop awareness of your psychological patterns and gradually transform your relationship to them.

It means being patient with yourself and others through the messy process of identity evolution. It doesn't happen on strategic timelines; it happens on psychological timelines, which are slower and less predictable.

It means accepting that you'll still have identity reactions even after you've done significant inner work. **The work doesn't eliminate your humanity; it just gives you more choice in how you respond to it.**

The Freedom on the Other Side

Let me tell you what becomes possible when you've done enough identity work to loosen the trap.

You can receive feedback without defensiveness because you're not protecting a fixed sense of self. You can change course without feeling like you're admitting failure because you're not attached to being right. You can experiment with new approaches without fear because your worth isn't tied to specific capabilities. You can see market signals clearly because they're not being filtered through identity-protective perceptions. You can respond to what's needed rather than what preserves your sense of self. You can let go of what's not working and embrace what's emerging.

This is genuine adaptability. Not as a skill set, but as a state of being. And it comes from doing the deep identity work that most leaders avoid because it's uncomfortable and doesn't look like traditional business development.

I can tell you from direct experience: the freedom on the other side of loosening identity attachment is profound. You're more effective, not less. You're more confident, not less. But it's a different kind of confidence, one based on present-moment responsiveness rather than past-identity preservation.

This is what the next section of this book addresses: the actual inner work required to build genuine adaptability. The neuroscience of how consciousness functions and can be developed. Why healing trauma is essential for clear perception. How to elevate awareness in yourself and your organisation.

Because here's the truth: stuck is an identity problem masquerading as a strategy problem. And solving it requires going deeper than most business thinking dares to go.

Let's go there together.

4 The Neuroscience of Adaptation

Let me tell you about a moment that fundamentally changed how I understand why adaptation is so difficult, not just for organisations but for human beings in general.

I was sitting in a neuroscience lab at a university, electrodes attached to my head, watching my own brain activity displayed on a series of monitors, and the researcher asked me to think about my restaurant business, specifically about the period just before it failed. As I began to revisit those months in my mind, the frantic energy, the mounting pressure, the constant sense that something was slipping away no matter how hard I worked, I could see the screen light up with activity in my amygdala and other threat response regions, while my prefrontal cortex, the part of the brain associated with reasoning, creativity, and complex problem solving, showed noticeably reduced activity.

The researcher looked at the data and said, almost casually, 'This is interesting. Your brain is essentially in survival mode when you think about that period. The very regions you would need for adaptive thinking are being suppressed by the threat response'.

That was the moment something truly clicked for me. I had not failed to adapt because I was not intelligent enough or because I did not care enough. I had failed to adapt because my brain was quite literally in the wrong state to adapt. I was trying to solve complex, strategic, forward-looking problems while my nervous system and my neurology were optimised for one thing only, survival, for fight, flight, or freeze.

What I have come to understand since then is that our awareness is far more shaped by our memories than we realise, and our perspective is far more shaped by the state of our brain than by our intentions. When you carry unprocessed experiences, unresolved stress, or emotional wounds, they do not sit quietly in the past; they live in the nervous system as triggers, and those triggers repeatedly push the brain into a defensive, reactive state. Over time, if that pattern is repeated often enough, the brain does not just visit that state; it learns it. It begins to treat anxiety, urgency, and threat as its default operating system, and from there your thinking becomes narrower, more rigid, more reactive, more focused on control and protection than on creativity or possibility.

This is why adaptation is not primarily a cognitive challenge; it is a neurological one. The state of your brain, moment by moment, determines what you can see, what you can imagine, what options even appear to exist for you. If your past is still running your nervous system and your nervous system is still stuck in survival, then no amount of intelligence, strategy, or willpower will give you access to truly clear, flexible, or forward-looking thinking. And this is the great blind spot of most business and leadership culture, because we behave as if better thinking is just a matter of trying harder, when in reality the quality of your thinking is determined by the state you are thinking from, and that state is being shaped, quietly and constantly, by layers of memory, emotion, and biology that sit far below the level of conscious control.

If you do not change that state, if you do not change your relationship to your past and to the patterns your nervous system has learned, then you do not really get to evolve, no matter how sophisticated your strategies look on paper, because you will keep trying to build the future from a brain that is still organised around surviving the past.

The Two Modes of Brain Function

Let me introduce you to a framework that's been transformative in my work with leaders and organisations. I learned about this from neuroscience research, but I've translated it into terms that are practically useful.

Your brain operates in different frequency states, measured in cycles per second called hertz. These aren't just abstract scientific measurements. They correspond to dramatically different modes of functioning that you experience every day, often without realising it.

The two states most relevant for our purposes are what neuroscientists call high beta and alpha.

High beta is characterised by rapid, intense brain wave activity, roughly 20–30 hertz. This is the state of doing, analysing, problem solving under pressure, defending, reacting. Your amygdala is highly active. Stress hormones like cortisol and adrenaline are elevated. Your prefrontal cortex, particularly the areas involved in creative thinking and perspective taking, shows reduced function.

In high beta, you're optimised for dealing with immediate threats and executing familiar responses. This is brilliant if you're actually facing a physical danger or if you're executing well-rehearsed tasks under time pressure.

But high beta is terrible for adaptation. In this state, your perception narrows. You focus on threats rather than opportunities. You default to familiar patterns rather than exploring new approaches. Your thinking becomes rigid and reactive. You grasp for certainty even when it's not available.

Alpha is a slower brain wave state, roughly 8–13 hertz. This is characterised by a calm, alert, open quality of awareness. Your prefrontal cortex is more active. Stress hormones are lower. You have better access to memory, creativity, and integrative thinking.

In alpha, you can see more possibilities. You can hold multiple perspectives simultaneously. You can notice patterns without being trapped by them. You can feel discomfort without immediately reacting to eliminate it. You're optimised for learning, creativity, and adaptive thinking.

The Buddhists have been talking about this for thousands of years, though they use different language. What they call the suffering mind is essentially high beta: the state of grasping, aversion, and reactivity that creates mental anguish. What they call the non-suffering mind is closer to alpha: the state of equanimity, presence, and clear seeing that allows for wise response.

Here's the crucial insight: most leaders and organisations are operating in high beta most of the time. The pressure, the urgency, the constant demands – they all push the brain into high beta and keep it there. And in that state, genuine adaptation becomes nearly impossible.

The Chronic High Beta Trap

Let me describe what chronic high beta looks like in practical terms, because I suspect you will recognise it immediately, not as something abstract or clinical but as the water most of us are swimming in every single day. You wake up already thinking about the day's challenges, your mind running ahead of you before your feet even touch the floor, rehearsing difficult conversations, scanning for problems, worrying about outcomes, while your body carries a background tension even though, objectively, nothing has happened yet. You move through your day in a state of controlled emergency; everything feels urgent, everything feels like it needs a response now, your attention is constantly being pulled across multiple streams, and even when you are with another person, part of your mind is already somewhere else, anticipating the next demand, the next message, the next fire to put out.

By the time evening arrives, you are exhausted but wired, your body tired but your mind still running at full speed, and sleep becomes a negotiation rather than a surrender because your nervous system no longer remembers how to downshift. You lie there replaying the day, worrying about tomorrow, unable to find genuine rest, and you start the next day not from renewal but from depletion. This is not just unpleasant; it is neurologically limiting, because in this chronic high beta state you literally cannot access the full capabilities of your brain, and the very regions you need for seeing new possibilities, for creative problem solving, for adaptive and integrative thinking, are being suppressed by the constant stress response.

I lived this way for years, and, like most people, I thought this was just what high performance looked like. I thought the pressure meant I was serious, committed, responsible, that this was simply the price of ambition and modern life, and I did not realise that I was systematically shrinking my own cognitive and emotional range. What makes chronic high beta so insidious is that it feels productive, because you are busy, you are responding, you are handling things, and there is even a certain adrenaline-fuelled aliveness that masquerades as engagement, but in reality it is a form of neurological impairment that has been so normalised in business and culture that we barely recognise it as a problem anymore.

I also believe, and this is a much bigger conversation and probably a whole book on its own, that this state is one of the reasons so many people are not falling in love anymore or are finding it so difficult to sustain deep, nourishing relationships, because when your nervous system is permanently in a state of urgency and defence, the idea of slowing down enough to truly see another human being, to open yourself emotionally, to tolerate vulnerability and uncertainty, feels almost impossible. On the other side of this, we are watching loneliness become an epidemic and anxiety become almost a default condition, and both are deeply connected to this chronic high beta way of living, even though we rarely talk about it in those terms.

I often hear people say, 'I suffer from anxiety', or 'I have ADHD', and while there are of course real clinical conditions, the uncomfortable truth is that for a huge number of people what they really have is an addiction to a high beta brainwave state, a nervous system that has been trained, educated, and conditioned for an older, slower, more linear world, now trying to survive inside a hyper-stimulated, always-on, constantly shifting one. It is not an accident that the sales of pharmaceutical mood enhancers and anxiety medications are doing better than ever, because in many cases people are simply trying to find some relief from the constant internal pressure, the constant background angst created by a brain that no longer knows how to come out of emergency mode.

And then we look at our children and wonder why they are so stressed, so anxious, so overwhelmed, and increasingly also medicated, forgetting the old line, 'Your actions are so loud,

I can't hear a word you're saying', because they are not learning this way of being from nowhere; they are watching us live it, model it, normalise it, and call it success. This chronic rush, this addiction to urgency, this high beta trance is not just shaping our organisations and our decision-making; it is quietly reshaping our relationships, our culture, and our inner lives in ways we are only beginning to understand.

The Familiarity Machine

There's another neurological reality we need to understand, one that quietly explains far more of our behaviour than most of us would like to admit, and that is this: by the time you are around 35 years old, various studies suggest you are having somewhere between 40,000, 60,000, and even up to 70,000 thoughts per day, and here's the part that should really make you pause, depending on how adaptive your brain is, somewhere between 70% and 90% of those thoughts are the same thoughts you had yesterday. Your brain, in other words, is not an adaptability machine; it is a familiarity machine, a beautifully efficient pattern-repeating system designed to conserve energy rather than to explore new territory.

This makes perfect sense from an evolutionary perspective, because the brain's primary job is not to make you happy or successful or enlightened; it is to keep you alive, and familiar patterns are safer and cheaper, metabolically speaking, than novel ones. Your nervous system has been shaped by millions of years of evolution to run automatic programmes, to default to what is known, to repeat what has worked before rather than experiment with what might work better, because in a world where threats were mostly physical and change was slow, this was not a bug, it was a feature. You did not want to be constantly philosophising about whether that rustle in the bushes might be a new kind of friendly creature; you wanted to react instantly based on past experience, and that bias towards the familiar kept our ancestors alive.

But in a world of exponential change, this same bias quietly turns into a liability, because your brain keeps trying to fit genuinely new situations into old categories, it keeps running yesterday's programmes to deal with today's challenges, and it keeps seeking the comfort of the known even when the known is clearly no longer working. You can see this not just in how we work, but even in something as simple and human as our taste in music, where research suggests that for most people their musical preferences largely stop evolving around the age of 35, which is why your parents never really liked your music and why you probably don't really like your kids' music, not because it is objectively worse but because your brain has become attuned to a certain set of patterns, tempos, and emotional textures, and anything outside of that starts to feel like noise rather than novelty.

This is also why adaptation feels so hard, why it takes so much energy, and why we so often find ourselves defaulting back to old patterns even when, intellectually, we know we want to change, because we are not just fighting habits or laziness, we are pushing against millions of years of neurological programming that is optimised for familiarity over adaptability. And to make matters worse, the educational systems and organisational structures most of us have grown up in have systematically reinforced this familiarity addiction rather than challenging it, because at school we were not really asked what we learned; we were asked whether we passed. At university we were not asked what we discovered; we were asked whether we got the degree. And at work it is rarely about exploration or creative risk; it is about hitting your numbers, and if you do not hit your numbers, nothing else really matters.

All of this has quietly produced a world full of people who think in linear, repetitive, familiar ways, and brains that are exquisitely optimised for predictability and repetition but deeply underprepared for the kind of adaptive, fluid, context-sensitive thinking that an exponentially changing world now demands.

Why You Can't Think Your Way Out

Here's something that frustrates many leaders when they first encounter this material: you cannot think your way out of a triggered state.

The very act of trying to think your way out keeps you in high beta. You're using analytical, problem solving, effortful cognition, which is precisely the mode that's limiting you. It's like trying to relax by tensing harder. The more you try, the more you reinforce the state you're trying to escape.

I watched this play out in my own experience during the restaurant crisis. I would recognise, intellectually, that I was stressed and reactive. I would tell myself to calm down, to think more clearly, to take a broader perspective. And then I would try very hard to do those things.

But trying hard is a high beta activity. My attempts to think my way to calmness were actually keeping me stuck in the stressed state. I was like someone trying to fall asleep by concentrating really hard on sleeping.

This is why so much business advice about stress management and clear thinking doesn't work. It treats the problem as cognitive when it's actually neurological. You can't cognitively override your brain state. You have to actually shift the state itself.

This requires different approaches: meditation, breathwork, somatic practices, sometimes deeper work like therapy or, in my case, plant medicine ceremonies. These work not because they give you better ideas but because they actually change your neurological state, shifting you from high beta to alpha where genuine clarity becomes possible.

The Power of Memory Reframing

Here's where the neuroscience gets genuinely hopeful, and where I want to share something transformative that I've experienced personally.

Your memories aren't fixed recordings of what happened. They're reconstructions, stories your brain tells about the past, and those stories can change.

Most people don't realise this. They think their memories are objective records, that what they remember is simply what happened. But neuroscience has shown us that memory is far more malleable than that. Every time you recall a memory, you're actually reconstructing it, and in that reconstruction, the memory can be modified, reinterpreted, even fundamentally changed.

This matters enormously for adaptation because our identities are built on our memories. Who you think you are is largely determined by the stories you tell about your past. And if those stories can change, so can your identity.

I experienced this in a profound way during a meditation retreat recently. I'd carried a particular story about my childhood for decades. My father could be volatile, sometimes violent. My mother stayed in the situation far longer than she should have. I'd built my identity around being someone who survived a difficult upbringing, someone who'd overcome adversity, someone who was always braced for things to fall apart because I'd watched them fall apart before.

That story was true. Those things happened. But it wasn't the only true story about my childhood.

During this retreat, in a very deep state of meditation, a state of genuine nothingness and openness, I was shown a different aspect of my upbringing that I'd completely forgotten. I was an exceptionally resilient and successful child. I did remarkably well at school, both academically and in sports. I was so advanced that I was promoted past certain grades, skipping from Standard One to Standard Three and then from Standard Four to Standard Six. This was a dramatic thing back then in South Africa, a recognition of my intelligence, capability, and resilience that very few children received.

I had forgotten this entirely. I'd spent so many years focused on the trauma, on what was wrong with my childhood, on my father's violence and my mother's acceptance of it, that I'd lost touch with what was also true: that I was an exceptional kid with remarkable resilience and ability.

When this memory resurfaced, everything shifted. I wasn't just someone who'd survived difficulty. I was someone with innate capability and resilience that had been evident from the very beginning. The trauma was real, but so was my strength. And I got to choose which story to centre my identity around.

What happened in that meditation was that I shifted my focus from one set of memories to another set of memories, both equally true, but with very different implications for who I understood myself to be. I changed what I remembered, and in doing so, I changed my future, because your future is very much determined by your past, by which version of your past you carry forward.

Your Friend's 40-Year Mistake

Let me tell you another story that illustrates this, one that a friend shared with me recently over lunch.

When he was 19 years old, he went for an interview at Maersk, the massive Danish shipping company. He was a shy kid, and this was a group interview, intimidating for anyone but especially for someone who didn't naturally speak up.

At one point, the person running the interview asked the candidates what type of people Maersk needed to hire. My friend surprised himself by actually answering. He stood up and said, 'Well, you're such a big organisation, you obviously need all types of people'.

The interviewer shut him down hard. 'No', he said dismissively. 'We need Maersk-type people'.

My friend spent the next 40 years angry with himself for opening his mouth when he shouldn't have. He berated himself for that moment constantly. It became part of his identity, a story about how he always said the wrong thing, how he should have stayed quiet, how he didn't belong in rooms like that.

Forty years of self-criticism based on one moment.

And then recently, as he got older and gained perspective, he realised something. The interviewer was wrong. Of course a massive global organisation needs all types of people. You can't run a company that size with only one type of person. His 19-year-old self had actually been right, and the interviewer had been narrow minded and dismissive.

In that moment of reframing, 40 years of self-criticism dissolved. The memory didn't change, but its meaning completely transformed. He wasn't someone who'd said the wrong thing. He was someone who'd had the courage to speak up with an insight that was actually correct and had simply encountered someone who wasn't ready to hear it.

This is available to all of us. The stories we tell about our past, the meanings we've assigned to our experiences, the identities we've built from our memories – they can all be re-examine and reframed.

What Ayahuasca Taught Me About Perception

I want to share something that might feel unusual in a book about leadership and adaptation, but it sits right at the centre of everything we're talking about, because it has to do with perception, with the state of your nervous system, and with the difference between living inside your patterns and being able to see them from the outside.

Circa 2016/2017 I went to Peru for an ayahuasca ceremony, not because I was looking for business insight but because I was heartbroken. A girlfriend had cheated on me, it had shaken me far more than I wanted to admit, and I was carrying that dull, heavy mix of anger, sadness, and confusion that comes when something personal collapses and you realise you don't actually understand your own reactions as well as you thought you did. I went there wanting answers about that relationship, about the pain, about why it had hit me the way it had. And very early in the ceremony, what came back was something completely unexpected. It was almost as if the medicine, or the intelligence behind the experience, said to me, very clearly, 'We're not here to talk about that. You still have work to do there. We want to talk to you about power'.

At the time, I had no idea what that meant. My first book was about to come out, I had no sense of what was coming, no idea it would become a bestseller, and no particular relationship to the idea of 'power' at all. And yet what followed was a message that has stayed with me ever since. It was explained to me that there are two rules to power. First, whatever access to insight, information, or understanding you are given is not for you alone; it is meant to be shared. Second, the moment you stop sharing, you stop receiving. That idea, about generosity and flow, about not hoarding insight as identity or status, has quietly shaped almost everything I've done since, from writing books to speaking to sharing ideas as openly as I can.

But that wasn't the deepest lesson of that experience. The deeper lesson was about perception itself. In that altered state, in a way that reminded me very much of what deep meditation can also do, I could suddenly see my own life, my own patterns, and my own reactions as if I were no longer trapped inside them, but standing just far enough outside to notice how they worked. It felt a bit like that old Matrix question: are you in the system, or are you able to look at the system? Are you inside your conditioning, or can you, at least occasionally, watch it operating?

What became painfully obvious is how much of what we call 'who I am' is actually a bundle of old memories, unhealed experiences, and protective strategies that are running the show without us realising it. I could see how fear makes us defensive, how the need for control makes us rigid, how old wounds quietly shape the way we interpret other people's intentions and the way we make decisions, and how easily we confuse these patterns with something like objective judgement or rational thinking. In other words, I could see that my perception in normal waking life was not neutral at all; it was filtered, narrowed, and biased by emotional history I hadn't fully processed.

This is why experiences like meditation, and yes, experiences like this too, can be so revealing, not because they give you some magical new information, but because they temporarily change the state of the system that is doing the perceiving. They move you, even briefly, out of the habitual, defensive, identity-driven mode of mind and into a wider, more spacious vantage point, where you can actually see how you've been seeing. And once you've seen that, you can't unsee it.

What I've come to believe, and what I keep seeing in leaders and organisations, is that this is almost always what's really going on when adaptation fails. It's not that people are stupid or lazy or even badly intentioned. It's that they are making decisions from inside a psychological and neurological state that is shaped by fear, by past experience, and by identity protection. The CEO who cannot pivot because their sense of self is fused with the current strategy, the leadership team that dismisses new ideas because they feel threatening rather than curious, the organisation that clings to a failing model because uncertainty feels more dangerous than slow decline – these are not primarily rational failures. They are perceptual ones.

And this is the real link between awareness, brain state, and adaptability. When you change the state from which you are seeing, you change what you are able to see. When you are no longer completely inside the Matrix of your own history and identity, even for a moment, you begin to realise how much of what you took to be 'reality' was actually interpretation. And from there, something genuinely new becomes possible, not because the world has changed but because you finally have.

Why This Matters for Adaptability

You might be wondering what memory reframing and altered states of consciousness have to do with organisational adaptability. The connection is direct and profound.

Your future is determined by your past. Not in some mystical sense, but neurologically. The way you perceive possibilities, the options you can see, the risks you're willing to take, the changes you can embrace – all of this is shaped by the memories and identity you're carrying.

If your identity is built on stories of limitation and fear, you'll approach the future with limitation and fear. If your identity is built on stories of resilience and capability, you'll approach the future with resilience and capability.

I've worked with leaders whose entire strategic outlook was shaped by one failure early in their career. That failure had become their dominant story about themselves, colouring every subsequent decision with excessive caution and risk aversion. They couldn't see opportunities clearly because their past was filtering their perception.

When we did the work of reframing those memories, of finding different meanings in those experiences, of building new identity stories, their capacity for adaptive thinking expanded dramatically. Not because they learned new skills or frameworks but because they freed themselves from the psychological constraints of their old stories.

This is the inner game of adaptation. It's not just about understanding neuroscience intellectually. It's about doing the practical work of healing your nervous system, elevating your brain state from chronic high beta to more alpha awareness, and reframing the memories and stories that have been limiting your identity and therefore your future.

The Foundation for Everything That Follows

We've covered substantial ground in this chapter. Let me bring it together.

First, your brain state determines what you can perceive and how you can think. In high beta, you're limited to reactive, familiar patterns. In alpha, you have access to creative, adaptive capabilities. Most leaders operate in chronic high beta and are therefore neurologically limited in their ability to adapt.

Second, your brain is wired for familiarity, not adaptability. By age 35, 80% of your thoughts are repeats from yesterday. You're fighting evolutionary programming when you try to think new thoughts and develop new patterns.

Third, you cannot think your way out of a triggered state. Cognitive effort keeps you in high beta. You need practices that actually shift your neurological state.

Fourth, your memories aren't fixed, and the stories you tell about your past shape your identity and therefore your future. By reframing memories and building new identity stories, you can expand your capacity for adaptive thinking.

Fifth, and this is the critical insight that underpins the next chapter: your adaptability quotient isn't measured only by how quickly you learn new things. It's also measured by how quickly you recover from being triggered. Because triggered states pull you into high beta, narrow your perception, and lock you into familiar patterns. The faster you can return to alpha state awareness, the more adaptive capacity you have.

This is the inner game. Not positive thinking or mindset tricks, but genuine neurological transformation. Not just understanding these concepts intellectually, but doing the practices that actually change your brain state and heal the triggers that keep pulling you into reactive patterns.

In the next chapter, I'm going to give you a practical tool for accelerating this work, something I call the Happy Mayor Game that has been transformative for me and the leaders I work with. But the foundation is what we've covered here: understanding that adaptation is a neurological challenge, not just a cognitive one, and that your memories and identity stories are far more malleable than you probably realise.

Your brain can change. Your stories can change. Your identity can change. And when they do, your capacity for genuine adaptability expands in ways that no strategy or framework can provide on its own.

That's the inner game. That's the foundation for everything that follows.

5 Healing Before Building

There's a question I get asked constantly by leaders, and it almost always comes wrapped in urgency and good intentions: 'Can't we just skip to the strategy part? I understand the psychology is important, but we've got a business to run, so we need to move quickly'. I understand that impulse deeply, because when your organisation is under pressure, when competitors are moving fast, when the board is asking uncomfortable questions, and when the numbers are no longer where you want them to be, spending time on inner work can feel like an indulgence you simply don't have the luxury to entertain.

But here's what I've learned, both from watching organisations struggle and from my own journey through change: trying to build new capabilities on top of unhealed patterns doesn't just fail; it often makes things worse. You end up with more sophisticated strategies being executed by more stressed, more reactive, more triggered people, which doesn't create clarity or momentum; it creates a more complex and more expensive version of the same dysfunction.

It's a bit like deciding you want a beautiful new hotel and trying to build it on top of the old one without ever tearing the old structure down. If the foundations are cracked, if the beams are compromised, if the plumbing and wiring are already failing, adding more floors and better furniture doesn't solve the problem; it just hides it for a while and makes the eventual collapse far more costly. At some point, you have to accept that you can't renovate your way out of a structural problem; you have to clear the site and rebuild properly.

Organisations are no different. You can't keep stacking new strategies, new structures, and new operating models on top of old, unexamined patterns and expect something genuinely new to emerge. If the foundations are built on fear, reactivity, unprocessed stress, and outdated identities, then whatever you build on top of them will eventually inherit the same weaknesses, no matter how modern or intelligent it looks on paper.

Let me tell you a story that illustrates why healing really does have to come before building.

The Executive Team That Couldn't Transform

I was brought in to work with the leadership team of a global professional services firm. They were facing significant disruption in their industry. Technology was automating much of their traditional work. Clients were demanding different engagement models. New competitors with different cost structures were taking market share.

The executive team understood the strategic challenges intellectually. They'd done extensive analysis. They'd developed a comprehensive transformation plan. They'd allocated resources. On paper, everything looked right.

But execution was going nowhere. Every initiative seemed to stall. Meetings that should have been about moving forward became debates about why things wouldn't work. Different executives were pulling in different directions. The transformation programme was consuming enormous energy whilst producing minimal results.

In my first few weeks working with them, I observed something fascinating. Whenever the conversation turned to fundamental change, to doing things differently rather than just better, the energy in the room would shift. People would become more defensive, more rigid. The quality of thinking would deteriorate. What had been strategic discussion would devolve into position defence.

They were getting triggered. All of them. In different ways, for different reasons, but the pattern was consistent.

The CEO had built her career on operational excellence. Her identity was 'the person who makes complex systems run smoothly'. Fundamental transformation threatened that identity, pushing her into a defensive state where she'd focus on all the reasons why proposed changes would create operational chaos.

The CFO had deep trauma around financial instability from his childhood. Any discussion of transformation spending, of investing before you could measure returns, would trigger intense anxiety. He'd become risk averse in ways that were completely disproportionate to the actual financial situation.

The head of client services had been burned badly in a previous transformation attempt at another firm. That experience had left her with deep scepticism about change initiatives. Any new proposal would trigger memories of that failure, making her resistant in ways she couldn't quite articulate.

The chief technology officer had spent 15 years building the current systems. Every discussion about replacing or fundamentally changing those systems felt like a personal attack on his life's work. He would intellectualise his resistance, framing it as technical concerns, but the underlying emotion was grief and fear.

None of this was visible to them. They thought they were having strategic disagreements. They thought they were being appropriately cautious. They didn't recognise that their own unhealed patterns were driving the dysfunction.

I had to make a difficult recommendation: before we went any further with the transformation strategy, the leadership team needed to do healing work. They needed to recognise and address their own triggers. They needed to develop enough consciousness to see when they were reactive rather than responsive.

The CEO looked at me like I'd suggested they all join a commune. 'We don't have time for therapy. We need to execute on our strategy'.

'You've been trying to execute for 18 months', I said gently. 'How's that working?'

That question landed. She was quiet for a long moment, then nodded slowly. 'Okay. What would this actually look like?'

What Unhealed Patterns Actually Look Like in Business

Most of the things that end up shaping our leadership don't announce themselves as wounds, and they certainly don't show up wearing the label of 'trauma'. They show up as urgency, as overworking, as control, as perfectionism, as an inability to rest, as a constant low-grade anxiety about things falling apart, as a need to prove something to someone who isn't even in the room anymore. They show up as patterns, as defaults, as the invisible emotional posture we bring into every decision, every conversation, every risk we take or avoid.

I only really began to understand this when I looked honestly at my own relationship with money, work, and success, and where it had actually come from. I grew up mostly with a single mom, and we were always financially challenged, even before my parents separated. My mother worked as a secretary, and she carried the entire weight of keeping my brother and me afloat on a salary that was never quite enough, and because she had no one else to share that stress with, I became the person who heard it, who felt it, who absorbed it. I'm endlessly grateful to her for what she did, but watching that constant strain, that quiet worry about bills and survival, left a very deep imprint in me.

Years later, I came across a line that stopped me in my tracks: 'Are you running away from the darkness, or are you running towards the light?' And I realised, with uncomfortable clarity, that I had never really been running towards wealth, success, or abundance. I had been running away from poverty. Even when I was doing well, even when I was building businesses, even when things looked ambitious and bold from the outside, the emotional engine underneath it all was fear, not excitement. I used to say it openly to customers in my restaurants, not 'I want to be rich', but 'I never want to be poor again'. And at the time, that sounded like motivation. In hindsight, it was anxiety in a very respectable suit.

From the outside, those two things look identical. Both people work hard. Both are driven. Both are focused and ambitious. But inside, they are living in completely different nervous systems. One is pulled forward by curiosity and possibility. The other is being chased by a memory.

And this is where it becomes deeply relevant to leadership and organisations, because you see this pattern everywhere. You see it in CEOs who are still trying to earn approval from a father who never gave it. You see it in founders who can't stop pushing because slowing down feels like danger. You see it in leaders who accumulate power, status, or money, not because they love the game, but because some younger version of them is still trying to feel safe, still trying to prove something, still trying to outrun a past that never got properly integrated.

These patterns don't stay personal. They shape strategy. They shape culture. They shape risk appetite, decision speed, how conflict is handled, what gets avoided, what gets overcontrolled, what gets forced. And because they live below awareness, they often run the show while we tell ourselves very sophisticated stories about vision, ambition, and growth.

This, more than almost anything else, is what determines whether a person or an organisation can truly see clearly and adapt, or whether they keep repeating the same behaviours in more and more complex forms. Not because they're incapable. Not because they're not smart enough. But because they're still running, quietly and tirelessly, from a past that never really let go of them.

The Adaptability Quotient: A Different Way to Think About Change

Over the years, I've come to see something that completely reframed how I understand adaptability, both in leaders and in organisations, and it's this: adaptability has far less to do with how fast you can learn something new, and far more to do with how quickly you can come back to yourself after you've been emotionally hijacked. In other words, your real Adaptability Quotient is not measured by how clever you are or how many new frameworks you can absorb; it's measured by how long you stay stuck after you've been triggered.

The moment you are triggered, your brain does something very specific and very predictable. It shifts into that high beta survival state we spoke about earlier. Your perception narrows. Your thinking becomes rigid. Your body moves into defence or attack. You don't see what is, you see what you're afraid of. And in that state, no matter how intelligent you are or how experienced you are, you simply cannot adapt. You can only react. And reaction, by definition, is the past replaying itself in the present. It's yesterday's nervous system trying to solve today's problem.

The real cost is not the trigger itself. The real cost is how long you stay there. If something takes you out for an hour, you've lost an hour of clear perception. If it takes you out for a day, you've lost a day of real thinking. If it takes you out for weeks or months, which happens far more often than most leaders would ever admit, then you've been living inside an old pattern while telling yourself you're being strategic.

What I've learned, both through my own inner work and through watching people closely, is that some people are not just triggered occasionally. Some people have been triggered for most of their lives. The original event is long gone, but the nervous system never updated, and over time that unhealed reaction doesn't just stay a reaction; it becomes temperament, then personality, then identity. If you're triggered for a week, you're just moody. We've all been there, stuck in a sulk bubble or an anger bubble. If you're triggered for two or three weeks, people start walking on eggshells around you. You're now 'difficult'. And if that state never really resolves, it starts to compound, quietly, invisibly, until you're no longer defending a moment; you're defending a whole life story you don't even realise you're living inside.

I became painfully aware of this after ayahuasca ceremonies, when I could suddenly see, from the outside, how many of the stories I told myself about people, about situations, about who I was, were not truth at all, but old emotional reactions that had been misread, frozen in place, and slowly assembled into a worldview. In those moments it became obvious that what we call personality is very often just a collection of unresolved triggers that have been rehearsed for so long they now feel like 'me'.

You can see this everywhere once you start looking for it. You see it in the perpetually angry man who is actually still defending an old wound. You see it in the perpetually sad person who is still mourning something they never processed. You see it culturally too. As a Middle Eastern person, I can say this with both affection and honesty, our grandmothers are almost always in pain, almost always suffering, and it's not because life is actively attacking them every day; it's because their nervous systems learned a long time ago that suffering and guilt are how love gets negotiated. There's a kind of reverse-bullying in it. Guilt becomes the currency of connection. I once watched a Greek comedian open his set by saying, 'I phoned my mother and said, Hi Mom, and she said, Who's this? I said, It's me, Stavros. She said, I used to have a son called Stavros, but he doesn't phone anymore'. And everyone laughed, because everyone recognised it. But underneath the humour is exactly the same pattern, unprocessed emotion turned into identity.

And this is not just personal. This is organisational. I've met executives who have been triggered for years without knowing it, operating from defensive patterns for so long that those patterns feel like character. They think they're being careful when they're being fearful. They think they're being strategic when they're being reactive. They think they're protecting the company when they're actually protecting an old wound.

Once you see this, you start seeing it everywhere. In difficult personalities. In broken cultures. In wars. In companies that implode for reasons nobody can quite explain. And the pattern is always the same. Our personalities are shaped by our brain states. Our brain states are shaped by our triggers. And our triggers are shaped by whatever never got metabolised, processed, and released.

This is why, in the end, adaptability is not a learning problem. It's a recovery problem. It's not about how fast you can move forward. It's about how fast you can come back from the past.

The Happy Mayor Game: A Ridiculously Effective Way to Recover from Triggers

So how do you actually get better at recovering from triggers, not in theory, not in a workshop sense, but in the messy, real moments when your chest is tight, your mind is racing, and you're about to send a message or make a decision you'll probably regret later? Over the years, after spending time with a wide range of teachers, therapists, meditators, and generally wise humans, and after collecting and curating a whole pile of ideas that actually worked in real life, I ended up stitching them together into something deceptively simple that has been quietly transformative for me and for a lot of the leaders I've shared it with. I call it the Happy Mayor Game.

The premise is simple enough to sound slightly ridiculous, which is usually a good sign. Imagine you are the mayor of your own inner city. Your job is not to eliminate citizens, suppress them, or throw them in jail; it is to keep the city calm, functional, and reasonably pleasant to live in. When there's unrest in the streets, when people start shouting or throwing emotional furniture at each other, you don't declare war on them. You listen, you mediate, you figure out what's actually going on, and you help the system settle.

Here's the part most people get wrong about being triggered. The parts of you that get reactive, defensive, anxious, or aggressive are not enemies. They are usually younger versions of you, often somewhere between six and fifteen years old, that were created during moments when life felt overwhelming and you needed a strategy to survive. Some learned to please everyone. Some learned to fight. Some learned to disappear. Some learned to be perfect. At the time, these were intelligent solutions. They worked.

The only problem is that these parts never got the memo that you grew up. So they're still running the same software. And when something in your current life even vaguely smells like the original danger, they jump into the driver's seat, grab the steering wheel, and start swerving. What they need is not to be overpowered. They need to be recognised, listened to, and gently informed that you are no longer nine years old; you have a credit card, a calendar, and a reasonable amount of life experience, and they can finally take a break.

So the game works like this. The moment you notice yourself getting triggered, and you will feel it in your body long before your mind admits anything is happening, you pause. You name what you're feeling. And then, instead of turning it into a philosophical problem, you turn it into a character. A citizen in your inner city. Giving them names helps. A lot.

Over time, I've met quite a colourful cast of characters in my own internal municipal government.

There's Marty the Martyr, who specialises in suffering nobly and imagining what terrible things everyone must be thinking about him. Marty has an extraordinary talent for turning neutral emails into personal attacks and awkward silences into proof of rejection. When Marty is running things, I feel wounded, misunderstood, and strangely committed to feeling sorry for myself.

Then there's Rocky. I met Rocky on a meditation retreat, which is a very strange place to meet someone who wants to punch people. Someone behind me was breathing in a way that I found. . .spiritually unacceptable, and I could feel the anger building, that familiar righteous heat rising in my chest, the urge to 'deal with the situation'. When I actually looked at the energy instead of just being inside it, I saw him clearly: an eight-year-old kid from a rough neighbourhood, somehow full of steroids, covered in pimples, permanently ready for a fight. Rocky thought he was protecting me. I had to sit him down, thank him for his service, and explain that attacking people for breathing loudly was no longer part of the strategic plan. I'm happy to report that Rocky retired that day, and nobody was harmed in the making of that retreat.

There's Unfair Freddy, who is constantly scanning the horizon for injustice, convinced someone else is getting a better deal. There's Shaky Sherman, who would prefer we all stay home forever because the world is clearly dangerous. And there's Courtney, who takes me to court daily, prosecuting me for crimes such as 'not being good enough', 'saying the wrong thing', and 'failing to be perfect'.

Courtney, by the way, took me about two or three days to work through when I first met her. That's how normalised some of these voices become. I was judging myself so constantly that I didn't even notice it was happening anymore. Once I named her, once I could see the pattern instead of just being inside it, the spell started to break.

The truly remarkable thing is this: most of these characters don't come back once they've been properly heard. Rocky is gone. Courtney is quiet. I was telling a friend about this game over dinner recently and realised I couldn't even remember all the names anymore, not because I'd forgotten the technique, but because the city has been. . .unusually peaceful.

And that's the real point. The goal is not to become a better manager of your triggers. The goal is to resolve them so they stop needing to exist at all.

How to Play the Game

Let me walk you through the practical steps of the Happy Mayor Game in a way that you can actually use in the middle of real life, not in some ideal, quiet, perfectly regulated moment, but in the moments when your chest is tight, your jaw is clenched, and you're halfway through typing a message you probably shouldn't send.

The first step is simply recognising that you're triggered, and this is far more subtle and far more difficult than it sounds, because when you are triggered, your entire system is convinced that your reaction is completely justified. The anger feels righteous. The fear feels intelligent. The defensiveness feels necessary. You don't feel 'off'; you feel correct. This is why the body is usually your best early warning system. Tightness in your chest or shoulders. Shallow breathing. Heat in your face. A clenched jaw. A restless, buzzing energy in your limbs. Long before your mind admits anything is happening, your nervous system is already telling you the truth.

The second step is to pause and name what is actually there, without trying to fix it, justify it, or improve it. Just ask yourself, as honestly as you can, what am I feeling right now? Am I angry? Afraid? Hurt? Ashamed? Defensive? Naming the emotion sounds simple, but it's powerful, because it begins to create the first bit of space between you and the reaction, and that space is everything.

This is also where that phrase you've probably heard a thousand times, 'You are not your thoughts', finally starts to become practical instead of philosophical. I heard that sentence for years and nodded wisely, but I had no idea what to do with it in the middle of a real emotional storm. What this game does is give you a way to actually experience that separation, not as an idea, but as a felt, physical shift in your body.

The third step is where the game becomes creative and, somewhat surprisingly, deeply effective. You visualise the triggered part of you as a character, not as an abstract feeling, but as a being. How old are they? What do they look like? How do they stand? What is their essential energy? And then you give them a name that captures their nature. The moment you do this, something subtle but profound happens. You no longer feel like the emotion. You can see it. It is no longer you. It is in front of you.

And I can tell you from experience, the moment I recognise one of my familiar characters and start reminding myself, 'Ah, this is Marty', or 'Here's Courtney again', my body almost immediately starts to soften. My breathing deepens. My shoulders drop. The charge begins to drain out of the system, because

I'm no longer inside the emotion; I'm in relationship with it. From that more objective place, I can actually love it, hear it, hold it, and treat it the way I would treat a frightened six-year-old version of myself, instead of arguing with it or trying to overpower it.

The fourth step is to communicate with the character in exactly that way, with warmth and respect rather than force. Remember, this is not an enemy; it is a younger part of you that learned its strategies in a time when you genuinely needed them. So you thank it for trying to protect you. You acknowledge that what it did once made sense. And then you gently, but clearly, let it know that you're an adult now, that you can handle this situation, that it doesn't need to work so hard anymore.

The fifth step is to let the system settle. In my own inner imagery, these parts often want to be held or comforted, and I frequently imagine them coming to sit on my lap and falling asleep, finally able to rest after years of standing guard. It might sound strange, but it works because it completes the emotional circuit. The part has been seen, acknowledged, thanked, and released from duty, and your nervous system understands that something has genuinely resolved.

At first, this process can take days and even weeks, especially with deeply embedded patterns. But the more you practice, the faster it goes. What once took days starts taking minutes. And eventually, with many triggers, it doesn't happen at all, not because you're better at suppressing them but because you've actually done the work and those parts no longer need to show up.

And that, ultimately, is the real goal. Not to manage your reactions forever but to outgrow them.

Your Natural State Is Peace

There's something important I need you to understand about this work: your natural state is peace, not craziness. The fact that you're being triggered is not a natural state. It's an unnatural state.

You can't be continuously in a bad mood and think that's normal. You can't be constantly reactive and defensive and think that's just your personality. Those are symptoms of unhealed triggers running programmes that were designed for circumstances that no longer exist.

When you start to meditate continuously, when you develop the practice of accessing alpha state awareness, your baseline shifts. You start operating from your heart rather than from your stressed mind. Because of that, you can continuously feel when you're going off track. The trigger points diminish dramatically. Your awareness of being triggered happens immediately.

And ultimately, you stop attracting the triggering scenarios into your life because you're not being triggered by them anymore. They become almost non-events. The situations that used to send you into days of reactivity barely register because you're not carrying the unhealed patterns that made them triggering in the first place.

This is the promise of this work: not just faster recovery from triggers, but actual healing that prevents the triggers from activating at all.

Why This Matters for Organisations

You might be thinking that all of this sounds useful on a personal level, but what does it really have to do with running a business, scaling a company, or leading an organisation through serious change. The honest answer is, everything, because organisations are not abstract entities. They are emotional systems made of people, and triggered people don't just create bad meetings; they create triggered cultures, reactive strategies, and companies that slowly lose their ability to think clearly.

When a CEO is operating from unhealed patterns, those patterns quietly shape every decision, every leadership conversation, every strategic priority, and every moment of pressure. When a leadership team is collectively triggered, the entire organisation begins to mirror that nervous system, and when key individuals cannot recover from their emotional reactions quickly, the whole system gradually loses its adaptive capacity without anyone quite knowing why. I've seen organisations remain stuck for years because a founder couldn't work through control issues, I've seen transformation programmes die because executives felt unconsciously threatened by anything that challenged their identity, and I've seen genuinely brilliant strategies collapse in execution simply because the people responsible for implementing them were operating from fear rather than from clarity.

You can see this pattern very clearly in the story of Uber. Under Travis Kalanick, the company's culture was aggressive, combative, hyper-competitive, and constantly on edge, a business that always seemed to be fighting something or trying to prove something, and when the internal audits and stories began to surface, they revealed an organisation riddled with fear, misogyny, political games, and deeply reactive behaviour. When Dara Khosrowshahi took over, calm, measured, and far more emotionally regulated, the tone of the entire company slowly began to change, not because the strategy suddenly became smarter but because the nervous system at the top had changed. The organisation became more professional, more stable, more capable of long-term thinking, and far less driven by unconscious emotional reactions, which shows you something important: culture is not shaped by posters on the wall; it is shaped by the emotional state of leadership.

This is why the fastest way to increase an organisation's adaptive capacity is not to rewrite the strategy deck but to increase the emotional resilience of its leaders, and the fastest way to increase emotional resilience is to heal the triggers that keep pulling people into reactive states. And the fastest way to heal triggers is to learn to recognise them, name them, and actually do the inner work of integration and release, rather than endlessly justifying them as personality traits.

This isn't a luxury that comes after the strategy work. It's the foundation that makes strategy work possible.

The Invitation to Inner Work

There is a quiet truth that sits underneath everything we have explored in this book so far, and it is captured beautifully in a simple line that has stayed with me for years: the only way out is in. If you want better decisions, clearer strategy, stronger leadership, and an organisation that can truly adapt, the path does not begin in the boardroom or the strategy deck; it begins inside your own nervous system, your own patterns, and your own unexamined reactions to the world.

Let me be honest with you, not in a dramatic way, but in a grounded and practical one: this kind of work is not always comfortable, because it asks you to notice the parts of yourself that have been running the show from behind the scenes, the triggers you have normalised into personality, the defensive strategies you have mistaken for strengths, and the old emotional patterns that quietly shape how you listen, how you decide, and how you lead. It takes courage to look at those things without flinching, and sometimes it can feel confronting or even painful, but what it gives you in return is something most leaders have been missing for a very long time, which is real inner freedom and real clarity.

The alternative, whether we like to admit it or not, is to spend your entire career operating from reactions you cannot see, making high-stakes decisions driven by old fears, and trying to lead change from the same level of awareness that keeps re-creating the same problems. It is to wonder why transformation never quite sticks, why the same tensions keep resurfacing, and why, despite all the intelligence and effort in the room, things somehow keep circling back to familiar patterns.

The leaders who choose to do this work, who commit to healing before building, who develop genuine emotional resilience through practices like the Happy Mayor Game and similar inner disciplines, do not just become more effective, they become more settled, more present, and more spacious inside themselves, and from that place they naturally begin to meet complexity, uncertainty, and pressure with clarity rather than reactivity. Their organisations change not only because strategies improve but because the quality of perception and presence at the top changes, and that shifts everything downstream.

You cannot solve a problem from the same level of awareness that created it, and you cannot build a truly adaptive future on top of unhealed inner structures. The real sequence is always the same: you go in first, you do the work, you clean up the lenses through which you see the world, and then when you come back out into strategy, decisions, and execution, everything begins to move differently and often far more easily.

In the next chapter, we will explore how this inner work extends beyond the individual and into the collective nervous system of an organisation, because true adaptability is not just personal; it is cultural and systemic. But it always starts here, with you, with your willingness to turn inward with curiosity rather than avoidance, to meet yourself honestly, and to discover for yourself what happens when you stop trying to change the world from the same inner place that keeps re-creating it.

So the real question is not whether this works. The real question is much simpler, and much more personal.

Are you willing?

6 The Organisational Nervous System

Most organisations do not have a culture. They have a nervous system. And like any nervous system, it determines how the body responds to pressure, to uncertainty, to opportunity, to threat, and to change long before any conscious strategy or clever slogan ever gets a chance to intervene. You can feel this the moment you walk into a company. Some places feel open, spacious, curious, alive. Others feel tight, tense, defensive, political, brittle. Nothing on the wall tells you this. No values statement explains it. Your nervous system picks it up instantly, because it is reading the nervous system of the organisation.

This is why the same person can be a hero in one environment and a complete failure in another, and why, if you have ever followed sport, you will have seen this play out in the most visible way possible. A player leaves one team as a superstar, carrying the hopes of the fans and the expectations of the board, and within months looks lost, hesitant, almost unrecognisable, as if their talent has somehow evaporated overnight. And then you see the opposite: a player who seemed average, even forgettable, suddenly moves into a new team and begins to shine, playing with freedom, confidence, and creativity, as if something inside them has finally been given permission to breathe. The easy explanation is form or luck or age, but the deeper truth is always the same. Different systems bring out different nervous systems in people. Different emotional climates give different parts of us permission to exist.

Organisations work in exactly the same way. We like to believe that performance is mostly about talent or intelligence or experience, but again and again what decides whether people thrive or wither is the emotional field they are operating in, the invisible atmosphere of safety or fear, openness or defensiveness, trust or control. Put a creative, thoughtful human into a fearful, reactive system, and they will either shrink or become political. Put an average human into a calm, coherent, well-held system, and they will often exceed every expectation you had of them.

This is also why most transformation efforts fail before they even begin. They aim at the surface, at structures, incentives, reporting lines, KPIs, strategies, and operating models, while leaving the underlying nervous system untouched. And then everyone is surprised when the old behaviours reappear inside the new structures, when the same politics, the same fear, the same silos, the same defensive decision-making quietly reconstitute themselves under new names and new PowerPoint decks.

You can see this most clearly in the way modern organisations relate to time. Most corporate calendars are not designed around thought or depth or quality of attention. They are designed around urgency. Back-to-back meetings. Permanent availability. A quiet addiction to being busy. A strange pride in being overwhelmed. I once saw a sign in an advertising agency that said, 'Everybody calm down; we're not saving lives here', and it was funny precisely because it was true and because nobody actually behaved as if it were true. The emotional tone of most organisations is low-grade emergency, as if everything is always about to break, as if the world will end if this quarter's numbers are missed, as if there is no room for reflection because reflection feels like irresponsibility in a system that is addicted to motion.

The tragedy is that this kind of environment does not produce better thinking. It produces more familiar thinking. It does not create intelligence. It creates reactivity. When there is no space in the calendar, there is no space in the mind. When there is no room for silence, there is no room for anything genuinely new to emerge. People end up doing more and more of yesterday's work, faster and faster, and calling it progress.

Lateral thinking, real creativity, and genuine strategic insight require something most organisations have quietly engineered out of existence: time, psychological safety, a calm nervous system, and permission to play without immediately justifying the outcome. This is not a philosophical luxury. It is a neurological requirement. A stressed system does not innovate. It defends.

This is why the physical and symbolic behaviours of leadership matter far more than most leaders realise. I once walked into a company where the CEO sat at the head of the table, physically elevated, posture rigid, the entire room subtly oriented around him, and every conversation felt like a performance. People spoke carefully. Disagreement was disguised. The organisation was technically successful but strangely brittle, always one bad quarter away from internal chaos. In another company, I walked into the boardroom and found the CEO sitting in the middle of a long table, relaxed, present, listening more than speaking. When I asked him why he did not take the head of the table, he said, almost casually, 'I avoid it whenever I can. The conversation is better when it doesn't revolve around me'. That company, interestingly enough, was not only calmer; it was more profitable, more resilient, and more creative. One system was built around ego and control. The other was built around coherence and trust. Same world. Same pressures. Completely different nervous systems.

If you want to understand how deeply this goes, look at what happened at Uber. Under Travis Kalanick, the company grew at a breathtaking pace, but the emotional climate was aggressive, combative, performative, and permanently on edge. The internal stories that eventually came out, of misogyny, of fear, of corners being cut, of people being rewarded for winning rather than for acting with integrity, were not accidents. They were expressions of the nervous system of the organisation, which in turn was a reflection of the nervous system of its leadership. When Dara Khosrowshahi took over, something subtle but profound changed. The language changed. The tone changed. The pace changed. The company did not suddenly become slow or soft, but it did become more human, more stable, more capable of self-correction. Same market. Same technology. Same scale. A different nervous system.

You see a similar story, in a quieter and more elegant way, in what happened at Microsoft under Satya Nadella. For years, Microsoft was powerful but internally competitive, fragmented, and strangely defensive for a company of its scale and influence. Nadella did not start with strategy. He started with culture, with empathy, with learning, with the idea that the organisation itself had to move from a know-it-all posture to a learn-it-all posture. What changed was not just what Microsoft did but how it felt to be inside Microsoft. The nervous system softened. The company became more curious, more collaborative, more open to partnership, and, not coincidentally, more innovative and more valuable.

This is not magic. It is biology.

Every organisation, whether it knows it or not, is constantly answering one fundamental question for its people: is it safe here to think, to speak, to experiment, to be wrong, to be honest? If the nervous system of the organisation answers no, people adapt in predictable ways. They become political. They hide. They manage impressions. They avoid risk. They optimise for survival rather than contribution. And from the outside, leadership often misreads this as a performance problem or an engagement problem or a capability problem, when it is actually a safety problem.

This is also why most people love the first few weeks in a new job. You arrive with energy, ideas, and a sense of possibility. You still belong to yourself. And then, slowly and almost imperceptibly, the nervous system of the organisation teaches you how to be there. What not to say. What not to challenge. What matters and what does not. Where the invisible lines are. And unless the system is exceptionally healthy, you eventually become part of the very pattern you once found confusing or frustrating.

The same dynamic explains why companies like Patagonia feel so different to most corporations. When the former CEO titled his book *Let My People Go Surfing*, he was not being poetic. He was describing a fundamentally different relationship to time, trust, and human motivation. Patagonia is not obsessed with the theatre of busyness. It does not pretend that constant urgency is the same thing as importance. It understands, perhaps intuitively, that people who are allowed to live full, sane, embodied lives bring better energy, better judgement, and better creativity to their work. This is not idealism. It is pragmatism at a deeper level.

Most companies, by contrast, are addicted to quarterly results, to constant measurement, to the illusion that everything that matters can be captured in a spreadsheet. And slowly, without anyone explicitly deciding it, the organisation becomes a machine that trains anxiety. It rewards speed over depth, certainty over curiosity, compliance over truth. And then we wonder why people are burned out, why innovation stalls, why every transformation feels like pushing a piano uphill.

The deeper truth is uncomfortable but simple. You cannot build an adaptive organisation on top of a fearful nervous system. You cannot ask people to think differently while the environment is silently telling them to stay safe, stay small, and stay within the lines. You cannot get creativity from a system that is optimised for control.

This is why awareness matters at an organisational level just as much as it matters at a personal one. An organisation's awareness is not what it says in its strategy documents. It is what it can tolerate emotionally. It is what can be spoken without punishment. It is what can be questioned without career risk. It is what can be tried without blame.

And this brings us to a deeply counterintuitive insight. Most organisations do not need more alignment. They need more aliveness. They do not need more compliance. They need more presence. They do not need people who are perfectly calibrated to yesterday's rules. They need people who are able to sense what is emerging and respond without panic.

This also reframes what leadership really is. Leadership is not the ability to have answers; it is the ability to hold the field in which better answers can emerge. It is not the ability to control outcomes. It is the ability to regulate the emotional system of the organisation so that intelligence can function.

When leaders are anxious, the organisation becomes anxious. When leaders are defensive, the organisation becomes political. When leaders are calm, curious, and grounded, something extraordinary happens. People begin to think again.

Conversations deepen. The quality of attention improves. And slowly, almost invisibly, the organisation's capacity to adapt increases.

This is not about being nice. It is about being coherent.

If Chapter 5 was about healing the individual nervous system, then this chapter is about recognising that organisations, too, have nervous systems, and that no amount of structural change will work if that system remains chronically activated, fearful, or rigid. Strategy does not fail because it is wrong. It fails because the system executing it cannot hold the level of uncertainty, creativity, and honesty that real change requires.

The uncomfortable implication is that most transformation work is backwards. We try to change behaviour before changing the field. We try to install new thinking before changing the emotional climate in which thinking happens. And then we are surprised when the old patterns return.

The invitation here is not to slow down for the sake of slowing down or to become vague or unambitious. It is to become precise about where real leverage lives. Real leverage lives in the nervous system of the organisation, in the invisible architecture of safety, trust, and presence that determines whether people are capable of more than just repeating the past.

In the end, the question is not whether your organisation has the right strategy. The question is whether it has the emotional and neurological capacity to outgrow the strategy it currently believes in. And that, far more than any operating model or transformation roadmap, is what will decide who thrives in the years ahead and who slowly, very efficiently, optimises themselves into irrelevance.

7 Today and Tomorrow Teams

Let me be precise about something that gets confused constantly: innovation and disruption are not the same thing. They are fundamentally different activities requiring fundamentally different capabilities.

Innovation is about making your current business model better. More efficient. More refined. Serving your existing customers more effectively. This is Today work.

When you improve your manufacturing process to reduce defects, that is innovation. When you enhance your customer service protocols, that is innovation. When you add features to your existing product that customers have requested, that is innovation.

Disruption is about making your current business model obsolete. It is about exploring business models that would cannibalise your existing revenue. It is about serving customers you do not currently serve or creating value in ways that do not fit your current structure. This is Tomorrow work.

When Netflix shifted from DVD rental to streaming, they were not innovating their DVD business. They were disrupting it. When Amazon launched AWS, they were not improving their retail operations. They were creating an entirely new business.

Here is what is critical: the skills required for innovation are fundamentally different from the skills required for disruption.

Innovation requires deep expertise in your current business. The best innovators are often your most experienced people who have spent years mastering the current model.

Disruption requires the ability to question everything about your current business. The best disruptors are often people who have not been conditioned by years in your current model.

Asking the same person to do both is like asking Serena Williams to also be an F1 driver. Both require extraordinary skill, but they are completely different capabilities.

The Boeing and the Jet Fighter

A Boeing A380 is optimised for efficiency, reliability, and scale. It can carry 600–700 people across oceans profitably.

A jet fighter is optimised for speed, manoeuvrability, and adaptability to rapidly changing conditions. It cannot carry 400 people. It serves an entirely different purpose.

Imagine trying to build a machine that is both. You would fail at both. You would create something that is a mediocre passenger plane and a terrible fighter jet.

This is exactly what most companies do when they try to drive innovation and disruption with the same team.

Your Today Team is your Boeing. They are optimised for running the current business efficiently, serving existing customers reliably, executing at scale. This is essential work. Without a functioning Today, you have no resources to invest in Tomorrow.

Your Tomorrow Team is your jet fighter. They are optimised for exploring what is emerging, testing new approaches, and making your current business model obsolete before someone else does.

You need both. But they cannot be the same people, in the same place, measured by the same metrics.

The Shein Revolution: A Case Study in Structural Adaptability

I want to share an example that illustrates this principle more powerfully than any other I have encountered. It is the story of Shein, the Chinese fashion company that has fundamentally disrupted the global apparel industry and how their approach differs from traditional fast fashion leaders like Zara.

For decades, Zara was considered the pinnacle of fast fashion innovation. They built their empire on what they called 'quick response' manufacturing, reducing the time from design to store shelf from months to weeks. They invested heavily in supply chain efficiency, opened thousands of stores worldwide, and became the world's largest fashion retailer, adding roughly 10,000 new styles annually to their thousands of stores. Their model was built on economies of scale: the more stores they operated, the more garments they could order, the lower their per unit costs, the higher their margins.

Then Shein appeared and rewrote every rule Zara had mastered.

Shein does not operate on economies of scale. They operate on what I call economies of learning. Instead of producing large batches of garments and hoping they sell, Shein produces tiny batches of hundreds of different designs, measures real-time customer response, and scales production only on the items that customers actually want. They release between roughly 10,000 new styles every single day. Not every week. Every day.

Here is what makes this relevant to our discussion of Today and Tomorrow Teams: Shein did not build this capability by asking their existing teams to think differently. They did not try to retrofit economies of learning onto an economies of scale organisation. They built an entirely new organisational structure from scratch, one designed around adaptability rather than efficiency.

Their supply chain is not optimised for cost per unit. It is optimised for speed of learning. Their technology is not designed to forecast demand more accurately. It is designed to detect demand as it emerges and respond in real time. Their people are not measured on how efficiently they execute a predetermined plan. They are measured on how quickly they can test, learn, and adapt.

Zara, by contrast, is still fundamentally a Today organisation trying to do Tomorrow work with Today structures. They have talented people, substantial resources, and genuine commitment to innovation. But their organisational architecture, their supply chains, their metrics, their culture, everything is optimised for economies of scale. When they try to compete with Shein's speed, they are asking a Boeing to dogfight with a jet fighter.

This is not about technology. It is not about having better AI or more advanced algorithms. It is about organisational structure. Shein's Tomorrow capabilities are not bolted onto a Today organisation. They are the organisation.

The lesson for established companies is not to become Shein. The lesson is that Tomorrow work requires Tomorrow structures. You cannot graft disruptive capabilities onto an organisation designed for operational excellence and expect them to flourish.

Why the Same People Cannot Do Both

I saw a version of this play out inside a global hotel group I was working with not too long ago, and it's stayed with me because it captures the problem so perfectly. The leadership team had decided that they needed a 'metaverse strategy', which already tells you something about the level of abstraction they were operating at, so they gathered their regional and functional heads into a series of workshops and asked them to imagine what the future of hospitality might look like in virtual worlds. On paper it sounded progressive. In reality it was almost surreal.

Here you had people who had gone to hotel school, who had spent their lives mastering human-to-human service, atmosphere, emotion, experience, and the subtle art of making someone feel welcome and looked after, being asked to suddenly become visionaries in virtual environments, AI, and immersive digital platforms. Within minutes, the conversation either collapsed back into today's operational constraints or floated off into vague, buzzword-filled fantasies. 'We could do something in the metaverse, but our current brand standards wouldn't allow it'. 'Our guests come to us for real experiences, not digital ones'. Or, on the other extreme, grand statements that nobody in the room had the slightest idea how to execute.

And then, inevitably, someone said my least favourite sentence in the corporate world: 'Let's all get together and think out the box'.

The problem is that in today's world, you can't think your way out of the box from inside the box. That idea made some sense in 1985, when change was slower and the future was still a variation of the past. Today, asking a room full of hospitality executives to 'think out the box' about the metaverse is effectively asking them to become, in an afternoon, competent in AI, data science, game engines, virtual economies, and human behaviour in digital spaces, none of which sits inside their training, their identity, or their nervous systems. So what happens instead is either a retreat back to what they already know, or a layer of fantasy thinking that never survives contact with reality.

What struck me most was not that they were struggling with the topic, that's completely human, but that the very way the question was being asked made it impossible to get a useful answer. They weren't being invited into a genuinely new way of seeing. They were being asked to stretch their existing minds beyond their natural limits, and then everyone was surprised when the conversation snapped back to the familiar. It was a perfect example of how organisations keep trying to use yesterday's thinking structures to explore tomorrow, and then wonder why they keep circling the same ideas.

We were trying to imagine a different future using a mental model built entirely around the present. It is like trying to design a jet fighter using Boeing engineering principles.

But there is something even deeper happening here, something connected to the emotional work we explored in earlier chapters.

When you have spent years building expertise in the current model, your identity becomes intertwined with that expertise. Your sense of competence, your professional standing, your value to the organisation – all of it is rooted in your mastery of how things work today. Asking you to imagine a world where that expertise becomes obsolete is not just an intellectual exercise. It is an emotional threat.

This is why your best Today people often become the most resistant Tomorrow thinkers. They have the most to lose. Their triggers get activated. Their inner characters show up, telling them stories about why change is dangerous, why the new approaches will not work, why they need to protect what they have built.

I have watched brilliant executives, people with decades of experience and genuine strategic insight, become completely blocked when asked to think about futures that would make their current expertise less valuable. It is not a failure of intelligence. It is a failure of emotional regulation in the face of identity threat.

What actually happens when you ask the same people to do both Today and Tomorrow work is that Today always wins. Not just because the urgent overwhelms the important. But because Today feels safe and Tomorrow feels threatening. People default to what they know, what is comfortable, what delivers visible results quickly and what does not activate their deepest fears about becoming irrelevant.

The Today Team: Excellence in Execution

The Today Team runs your current business. They serve existing customers with existing products through existing channels. They optimise operations, improve efficiency, reduce costs, and enhance quality.

This is not maintenance work. This is the work that generates the revenue and profit that funds everything else. Without a strong Today Team, you have no Tomorrow.

The Today Team deserves respect, resources, and clarity about their mandate. Their job is to execute brilliantly on the current model. To serve customers exceptionally well. To operate efficiently and profitably.

What they should NOT be responsible for is disrupting themselves. They should not be measured on how well they are preparing for a future that makes their current work obsolete.

When you give the Today Team a clear mandate and remove the cognitive dissonance of being told to both optimise today and disrupt it, something remarkable happens. They get better at what they do. They take pride in operational excellence. They develop mastery.

Think about Zara's teams. These are exceptionally capable people who have built one of the most successful retail operations in history. They should not feel like failures because they cannot match Shein's speed. That is not their job. Their job is to execute brilliantly on Zara's current model whilst a separate Tomorrow Team explores what comes next.

The Tomorrow Team: Licensed to Disrupt

The Tomorrow Team's mandate is to make your current business model obsolete before someone else does. To explore business models that do not fit your current structure. To experiment with approaches that would cannibalise your existing revenue.

This requires a completely different type of person than your Today Team.

Your best Today people are often terrible Tomorrow people. They know the current business too well. They are too invested in current success. They see all the reasons why new approaches will not work based on current constraints.

The right Tomorrow people have different characteristics:

- They are comfortable with uncertainty. They do not need clear answers before they explore questions.
- They are willing to question sacred cows. They do not accept 'that is how we have always done it' as valid reasoning.

They can think in long time horizons. They are not worried about this quarter's numbers. They are exploring what might be true in three to five years.

They are comfortable with failure. Most Tomorrow experiments will not work. Tomorrow people see failed experiments as valuable learning.

They can synthesise across domains. They draw insights from adjacent industries, from technology trends, from societal shifts.

Often, the best Tomorrow people are *not* your most experienced executives. They are younger people who have not been conditioned by decades in the current model. They are people from adjacent industries who bring fresh perspectives. They are the people who, when told 'That is not how we do things here', respond with 'But what if we did?'

Different Buildings, Different Worlds

Here is something that surprises people: the Tomorrow Team should not be in the same building as the Today Team.

Physical separation matters more than you might think.

When Tomorrow people sit near Today people, they get pulled into Today thinking. Someone walks by with a customer crisis. They get invited to operational meetings. They start to feel guilty for exploring future possibilities whilst colleagues are fighting fires.

The Today culture is powerful. It is urgent. It is reinforced by immediate feedback loops and clear metrics. It will overwhelm Tomorrow culture if they are in proximity.

The Tomorrow people would ride the lift past all the floors where Today work was happening. They would run into Today colleagues who would ask what they were working on. They would get pulled into Today meetings. The physical proximity kept them tethered to Today thinking.

Move the Tomorrow Team to a completely different building across town. Suddenly, they were liberated. They were not constantly explaining themselves. They were not feeling guilty. They could build their own culture without Today's culture overwhelming it.

The separation is not about isolation. It is about protection. Protecting Tomorrow thinking from the gravitational pull of Today urgency.

Different Metrics, Different Timeframes

You cannot measure Tomorrow Teams with Today metrics. You cannot ask them about ROI in the next quarter. Tomorrow metrics are fundamentally different:

Quality of learning: What are we discovering about how the world is changing? What have we learnt from experiments?

Portfolio of options: What capabilities are we building that might be valuable in different future scenarios?

Early signals: What weak signals are we detecting that suggest emerging trends?

Strategic readiness: If our current business model became obsolete tomorrow, how prepared would we be to shift?

These are not soft metrics. They are rigorous. But they are oriented towards long-term adaptability rather than short-term performance.

The Adjacent Possible

Tomorrow work is not about predicting the distant future. It is about exploring what I call the 'adjacent possible'.

The adjacent possible is what is next to current reality. The emerging technologies that are just becoming feasible. The changing customer behaviours just starting to show up in your data. The new business models working in adjacent industries but have not arrived in yours yet.

This is where Tomorrow Teams should focus. Not on what might be possible in twenty years, but on what is becoming possible in the next three to five years that would disrupt your current model.

That is the sweet spot for Tomorrow work. Close enough to current reality to be credible and actionable. Far enough to be genuinely disruptive.

The Transition Layer

If Today and Tomorrow really are two different worlds, often with different people, different languages, different buildings, and very different success metrics, then the most important question is not whether they both exist, but how they are allowed to talk to each other without destroying each other. You cannot let them operate in total isolation, because then Tomorrow becomes irrelevant science fiction and Today becomes a perfectly run machine driving straight into obsolescence. But you also cannot simply have Tomorrow present their ideas to Today and expect Today to 'implement', because that almost always triggers an immune response. Today's world is built around reliability, efficiency, risk management, and quarterly performance, so when

Tomorrow walks in with ideas that are uncertain, half formed, and often threatening to existing structures, the natural reaction is to label them as impractical, disconnected from reality, or dangerous, and then quietly kill them.

What does work is creating explicit translation roles, people or small teams whose only job is to live in between these two worlds and help them understand each other. Their role is not to own Today and not to own Tomorrow but to continuously translate Tomorrow's insights into implications for Today's decisions and, just as importantly, to translate Today's constraints back to Tomorrow so that exploration does not become pure fantasy. I once saw this formalised in a company through a small group called the Horizon Scouts, and their mandate was beautifully simple and incredibly powerful. They tracked what Tomorrow was learning, what signals were emerging, what technologies or behaviours were starting to matter, and then they worked with Today's leaders to ask a very different set of questions, not 'How do we implement this now?' but 'If this becomes mainstream, what would it break?' 'What capabilities would we need?' 'What should we start quietly preparing for, even if we do nothing visible yet?'

The magic here is that this is not about immediate execution; it is about progressive readiness. Today continues to execute brilliantly in the present, but at the same time it starts, almost imperceptibly, to build the muscles that Tomorrow is signalling will be needed. By the time disruption actually arrives, it feels less like a shock and more like a door that has been slowly opening in the background, because the organisation has been preparing itself in small, intelligent, nondramatic ways.

But, and this is important, this translation model is not always enough on its own.

There are entire categories of change where simply translating insights back to Today is not only insufficient; it is almost pointless. When you start to look at things like zero marginal cost dynamics, where digitisation turns entire industries into something closer to software, as happened with music, communication, photography, media, and entertainment, you realise that some sectors do not just need to adapt; they need to be rebuilt. Transportation is a good example. Once you truly understand where autonomy, platforms, and software are taking mobility, it becomes obvious that you are not in the business of selling cars anymore; you are in the business of selling mobility subscriptions. That is not an 'improvement' to the existing model; it is a different game altogether.

In cases like this, bringing the idea back to the Today organisation as a discussion point is often useless, or worse, actively destructive, because the existing system is structurally and emotionally invested in a world that is about to disappear. Here, what you need instead is the ability for Tomorrow to spawn its own implementation teams, protected spaces where entirely new models can be built, tested, and iterated without being constantly pulled back into the logic, incentives, and nervous system of the old organisation. These are not innovation labs that report into Today. They are embryonic future businesses that may, over time, replace Today altogether.

So in practice, mature organisations need both. They need a Translation Layer that helps Today slowly prepare for plausible futures, and they also need the courage, in certain cases, to let

Tomorrow build independently, without asking for permission from a system that cannot yet understand what is being created. Which path you take depends on the sector, the speed of change, the maturity of the technology, the position on the hype cycle, and, most of all, on how existential the shift really is.

The real skill of leadership in this era is not choosing one of these approaches dogmatically, but learning to sense which kind of future you are dealing with, and then designing the right bridge, or the right separation, accordingly.

The Resource Question

For most established organisations, Tomorrow should be roughly 10–15% of your total workforce. Much less than that, and Tomorrow does not have enough resources to genuinely explore. Much more than that, and you are potentially weakening Today execution.

But here is what matters more: Tomorrow needs protected resources. Resources that Today cannot raid when there is pressure.

I have seen what happens when Tomorrow resources are not protected. Quarter gets tough. CFO looks at people exploring Tomorrow and says, 'We need them working on Today revenue'. Tomorrow gets reassigned. Tomorrow work stops.

Then next quarter, someone says, 'We should restart Tomorrow work'. You rebuild the team. Then the next pressure hits, and the cycle repeats.

You never build real Tomorrow capability this way.

The organisations that succeed make Tomorrow resources untouchable. The CEO explicitly protects them. 'Tomorrow budget is not available for Today pressures'.

This requires courage. It requires believing that long-term adaptability is more important than short-term performance smoothing.

The Leadership Requirement

None of this works without leadership that genuinely understands and protects the framework.

Most leaders say they want Tomorrow work. But when pressure hits, they instinctively pull all resources into Today.

Leaders who make this work do several things consistently:

They talk about Tomorrow as much as Today. In board meetings, in all hands gatherings, Tomorrow gets significant attention.

They celebrate Tomorrow learning, not just Today achievement. When Tomorrow runs an experiment that 'fails', they treat it as valuable.

They protect Tomorrow from Today pressure. When the CFO wants to raid Tomorrow resources, they say no.

They personally spend time with Tomorrow. Not just in formal reviews, but in real exploration. They visit Tomorrow workspaces. They participate in Tomorrow experiments.

This sends an unmistakable message: Tomorrow matters. It is central to our future success.

What This Framework Delivers

After 18 months of implementing this framework, that Munich company launched a new services division built entirely on capabilities the Tomorrow Team had developed. It did not feel like dramatic transformation. It felt like natural evolution because Today had been gradually preparing whilst Tomorrow built.

Meanwhile, Today operations had improved significantly. The discipline of focusing on operational excellence within a clear mandate led to real improvements in efficiency and customer satisfaction.

This is what the Today and Tomorrow framework enables when implemented with real commitment. Not overnight transformation, but systematic building of adaptive capacity whilst maintaining operational excellence.

The structure is straightforward: separate Today and Tomorrow. Different people, different locations, different metrics. Create translation mechanisms. Protect Tomorrow resources.

The difficulty is in the implementation, because it requires letting go of deeply held beliefs about how organisations should work. You have to accept that your best people should not do both Today and Tomorrow. That everyone should not be thinking about the future. That Tomorrow work will not show immediate returns.

But based on everything I have seen, this framework is the most reliable path to building genuine adaptive capacity. To thriving in exponential change rather than just surviving it.

The question is whether you are willing to implement it. Not just intellectually agree with it, but actually restructure your organisation around it.

Because the Speed Mismatch is not going away. The companies that survive will be those that can genuinely hold both Today and Tomorrow at the same time. Through conscious structural design that makes both Today excellence and Tomorrow exploration possible.

In the next chapter, I will show you how to deploy AI across both Today and Tomorrow using a simple strategic framework. And we will return to Shein to see how their structure maps onto a tool that can help you make sense of where and how to invest in artificial intelligence.

8

Simplifying Strategy

Complexity is the enemy of execution.

I developed the AI Strategy Scanner because I kept seeing the same pattern across almost every organisation I worked with. Leaders were drowning in information. Market reports. Competitor analyses. Technology assessments. Customer research. Board presentations. Consultant recommendations. There was no shortage of insight, no shortage of data, no shortage of opinions, and yet there was a very real shortage of movement.

Everyone was talking about AI. Everyone knew it mattered. But almost nobody could figure out what to actually do about it.

I would sit in strategy meetings where executives would debate for hours about AI adoption. Should we build or buy? Which use cases matter most? Which platforms should we bet on? How do we measure success? How fast is fast enough? The conversations would loop endlessly, consuming enormous amounts of time and energy, while producing very little clarity and even less decisive action.

The problem was not a lack of intelligence, and it certainly was not a lack of effort. The problem was overwhelm.

There were simply too many possibilities, too many data points, too many variables, too many things that could go wrong. And when the human brain is faced with that level of complexity, something very predictable happens. When information enters our mental space and it does not fit neatly into our existing understanding of the world, we do not calmly and rationally integrate it. We delete it. We distort it. Or we generalise it into something familiar and therefore less threatening. And we do this automatically, without even realising it, because the brain is always trying to conserve energy and reduce cognitive load, always trying to avoid having to build entirely new mental models from scratch.

This is not a flaw in the human mind. It is a survival feature. But in times of deep technological and strategic transition, it becomes a liability.

It is exactly what happened in the German automotive industry. Those companies were not stupid. They were not lazy. They were not asleep at the wheel. The shift from combustion engines to batteries, from mechanical engineering to software, from cars to mobility platforms, was not just a product change; it was a completely different worldview. The complexity of battery development, supply chains, and software ecosystems, as well as a totally different concept of what a car even is, was simply too far outside their existing mental models to engage with properly. So, like all humans do, they filtered it, simplified it, and quietly assumed it could be dealt with later.

By the time later arrived, it was already late.

They did not fail because they lacked data. They failed because the data did not fit into a simple, usable framework that allowed them to act before the pressure became existential.

This is what happens when leaders cannot see the forest for the trees.

Strategy, in many organisations, has become the opposite of what it is supposed to be. Instead of creating clarity that enables decision-making, it has become a factory for producing complexity that paralyses action. The more uncertain the world becomes, the thicker the slide decks get, the more sophisticated the language becomes, and the less movement actually happens.

That is why I created the AI Strategy Scanner, not to add more complexity but to cut through it.

Not to give leaders more things to think about, but to give them a way to think clearly about the things that actually matter.

It is a simple, rigorous framework for deciding where and how to deploy AI, how to build and separate their Today and Tomorrow Teams, and how to make sure they are not blindsided by futures they were psychologically unable to process.

Had the German car industry been working with a clear Today and Tomorrow structure and had they been using a framework like the AI Strategy Scanner, they would not have needed to predict the future perfectly. They would simply have needed to prepare for more than one plausible version of it.

That is all this is really about. Not certainty. Not prediction. Preparation.

Let me show you how it works.

The Fundamental Question

Before we get to the Scanner itself, you need to answer one fundamental question about your relationship with AI: are you going to be Defending, Extending, or Upending?

Defending means making your existing business more efficient but not really changing too many functions. You are using AI to do what you already do, just better and cheaper. This is the safest approach, but it is also the most vulnerable because you are not fundamentally adapting to how AI is changing the game.

Extending means changing how you deliver your core offering and benefiting your clients in a huge way. You are using AI to transform the customer experience or your operational capabilities whilst staying in your current business. This is about being significantly better, not just incrementally better.

Upending means you are going to upend your organisation and disrupt your industry or even create a new one. You are using AI to play an entirely different game, potentially making your current business model obsolete before someone else does.

Most organisations default to Defending because it feels safe. But in a world where AI is advancing exponentially, Defending is often the riskiest strategy because you are optimising for a game that is disappearing.

The right answer depends on your industry, your position, your capabilities, and your courage. But you need to make a conscious choice rather than drift into Defending by default.

The AI Strategy Scanner Framework

Once you have decided your stance, the Scanner helps you determine where and how to deploy AI across four distinct quadrants.

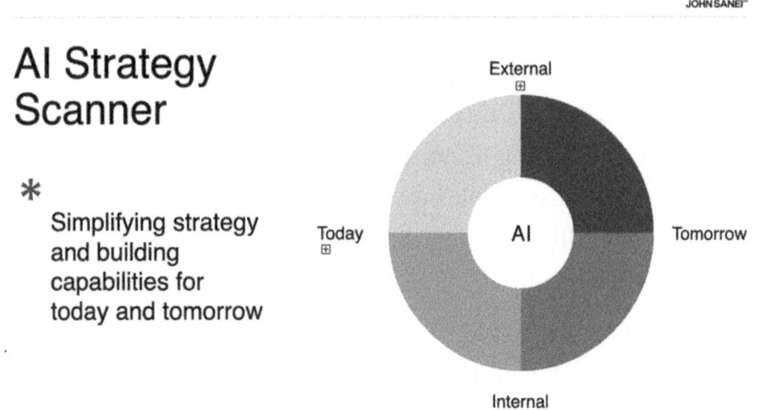

The framework is built on two dimensions:

Today vs. Tomorrow: Are you using AI to improve current operations or build future capabilities?

Internal vs. External: Are you using AI to enhance your internal operations or create external value for customers?

This creates four quadrants, each requiring different approaches, different teams, different metrics, and different expectations.

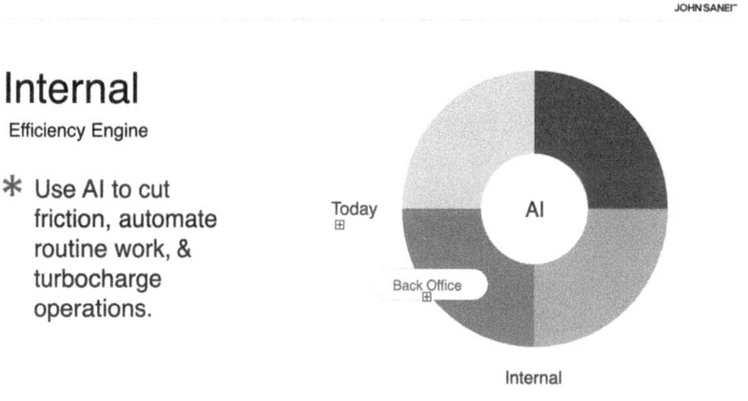

Quadrant 1: Today + Internal = Efficiency Engine

This is your back office. Use AI to cut friction, automate routine work, and turbocharge operations.

This quadrant is about Defending well. Taking the work that already happens internally and making it faster, cheaper, more accurate. Document processing. Data entry. Scheduling. Compliance checking. All the operational work that is necessary but not differentiating.

The beauty of this quadrant is that the ROI is usually clear and immediate. You can measure time saved, costs reduced, errors eliminated. This makes it easy to justify investment and demonstrate value.

Omega Healthcare provides a perfect example. Using AI-powered document understanding, they automated medical billing and insurance claims, processing more than 100 million transactions, saving 15,000 employee hours per month, cutting turnaround by 50%, and achieving 99.5% accuracy.

That is the power of the Efficiency Engine. You are not changing what you do. You are dramatically improving how you do it.

This is Today Team work. These are people who understand your current operations deeply and can identify where AI can eliminate friction and boost performance.

JOHNSANEI

External

Delight in Every Interaction

* Use AI to surprise and delight customers in unexpected & personalised ways.

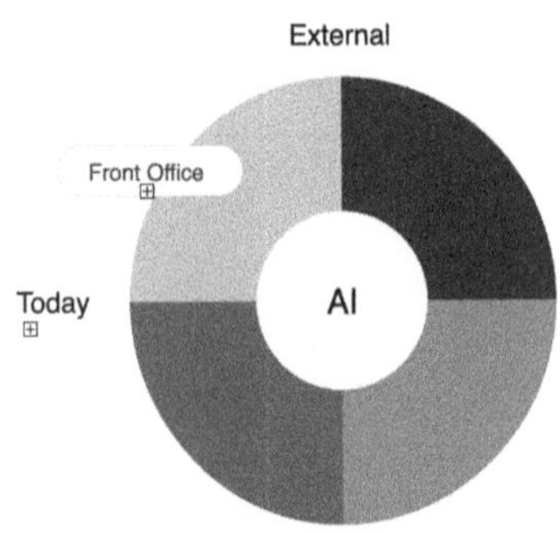

Quadrant 2: Today + External = Delight in Every Interaction

This is your front office. Use AI to surprise and delight customers in unexpected and personalised ways.

This quadrant is about Extending through exceptional customer experience. You are still serving your current customers with your current offerings, but AI enables you to do it in ways that feel magical.

Personalisation at scale. Anticipating needs before customers articulate them. Contextual interactions that feel remarkably human despite being AI powered. Creating moments of delight that build loyalty and differentiation.

Starbucks demonstrates this brilliantly. They leverage AI with contextual triggers like weather or time of day to push hyper personalised promotions. Suggesting a frappuccino during a heatwave. A hot coffee on a cold morning. These are not random offers. They are precisely timed, contextually relevant suggestions that drive both delight and sales.

The key here is that AI enables you to treat every customer as an individual at scale. Something that was impossible before.

This is also Today Team work, but it requires people who deeply understand customer needs and can imagine how AI might create better experiences. It is not just about efficiency. It is about emotion and connection.

JOHN SANEI

Internal
AI-Powered Evolution

* Use AI to reshape your flagship products or services from the inside out.

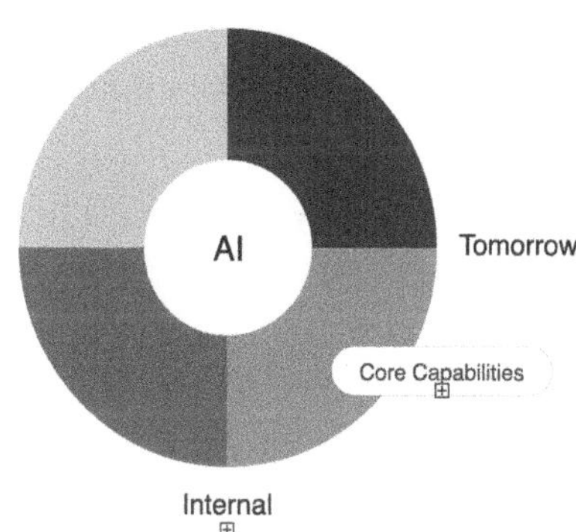

Quadrant 3: Tomorrow + Internal = AI-Powered Evolution

This is your core capabilities. Use AI to reshape your flagship products or services from the inside out.

This quadrant is about Extending or Upending your core offering. You are not just using AI to support what you do. You are using AI to fundamentally transform what you deliver.

This is where AI becomes embedded in your product or service itself. Where your capabilities become impossible without AI. Where the quality, speed, or scope of what you offer is transformed by AI at the core.

Pharma.AI in Hong Kong exemplifies this. This company introduced nine new drugs in its inaugural year, surpassing big pharma's typical launch rate of four to five. How? By using AI to simulate and predict drug interactions, dramatically reducing the need for expensive and time consuming human trials.

AI did not just make their drug development more efficient. It made their entire approach fundamentally different. They are playing a different game than traditional pharmaceutical companies.

This is Tomorrow Team work. These are people exploring how AI can transform your core capabilities in ways that were not previously possible. They are building the new version of your business whilst Today keeps the current version running.

JOHN SANEI

External

AI-Born Industries

* Use AI to launch entirely new business models or even categories.

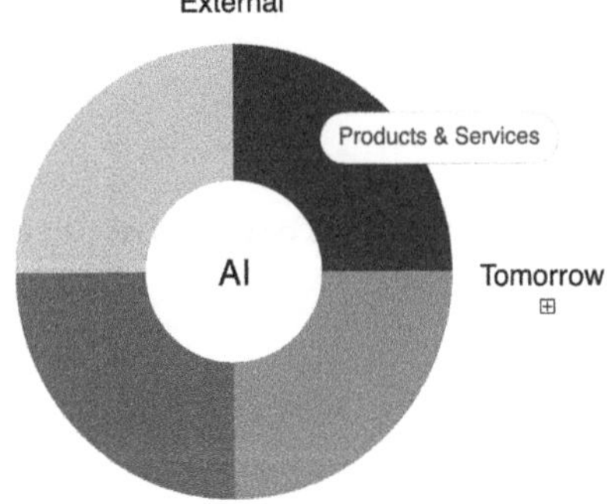

Quadrant 4: Tomorrow + External = AI-Born Industries

This is your products and services. Use AI to launch entirely new business models or even categories.

This quadrant is pure Upending. You are not improving existing offerings. You are creating entirely new ones that could not exist without AI. You are potentially creating new industries or redefining existing ones.

Built Robotics demonstrates this powerfully. They are pioneering fully autonomous heavy construction equipment with AI driven exosystem kits. They are not making construction equipment more efficient. They are creating a new category: robotic construction. They are disrupting how infrastructure gets built.

This is the highest risk and highest potential return quadrant. Many attempts here will fail. But the ones that succeed can create entirely new markets and businesses.

This is Tomorrow Team work at its most exploratory. These are people who can imagine entirely new possibilities, not just improvements to current approaches. They are building businesses that do not exist yet.

Shein Through the Scanner: A Master Class in Full Spectrum Deployment

In the previous chapter, I introduced Shein as an example of a company built from the ground up around economies of learning rather than economies of scale. Now I want to show you something remarkable: Shein does not just operate in one or two quadrants of the Scanner. They operate effectively across all four simultaneously.

This is what separates truly adaptive organisations from those merely experimenting with AI.

Shein in Quadrant 1: Their Efficiency Engine runs on AI-powered supply chain management that most traditional retailers cannot comprehend. Their systems automatically manage inventory across thousands of suppliers, optimise logistics in real time, and coordinate production across a distributed manufacturing network. They have eliminated the human bottlenecks that slow down traditional fashion supply chains.

Shein in Quadrant 2: Customer delight is not an afterthought for Shein. Their app uses AI to create hyper personalised shopping experiences, showing each customer a different storefront based on their browsing history, purchase patterns, body type, and style preferences. They do not just recommend products. They create the feeling that the entire store was designed specifically for you.

Shein in Quadrant 3: This is where Shein truly differentiates. Their core capability, the thing that makes them Shein, is AI-powered trend detection and rapid response manufacturing. Traditional fashion companies design a collection, manufacture it, ship it to stores, and hope customers want it. Shein's AI monitors social media, search trends, and customer behaviour in real time, identifies emerging micro trends before they peak, and triggers production of new designs within days. The AI is not supporting their business. The AI is their business.

Shein in Quadrant 4: Perhaps most impressively, Shein is using their AI capabilities to create entirely new business

> models. They have launched a marketplace platform that allows third-party sellers to tap into their AI-powered trend detection and manufacturing network. They are not just selling clothes anymore. They are selling access to an adaptive supply chain infrastructure.

Compare this to how Zara deploys AI. Zara uses AI primarily in Quadrant 1 for supply chain efficiency and inventory management, and somewhat in Quadrant 2 for customer analytics. But their core business model, the actual way they create and sell fashion, remains fundamentally unchanged. Their AI supports the business. It does not transform it.

This is the difference between using AI and becoming an AI-powered organisation.

The lesson is not that every company needs to be Shein. The lesson is that the Scanner can help you see where you are deploying AI, where you are not, and what that says about your strategic stance.

How the Quadrants Work Together

Here is what is crucial: you need activity in all four quadrants, but in different proportions depending on your strategy.

If you are Defending, you will concentrate heavily in Quadrants 1 and 2. Using AI to be more efficient internally and more delightful externally, but not fundamentally changing your business model.

If you are Extending, you will balance across Quadrants 1, 2, and 3. Using AI for efficiency and customer experience whilst also transforming your core capabilities.

If you are Upending, you will invest significantly in Quadrants 3 and 4 whilst maintaining enough in Quadrants 1 and 2 to keep the current business healthy enough to fund the transformation.

Most organisations make the mistake of only working in Quadrants 1 and 2. They use AI for efficiency and customer experience but never explore how it might transform their core capabilities or create entirely new businesses. They are Defending when the world demands Extending or Upending.

Mapping Your Today and Tomorrow Teams

The Scanner becomes even more powerful when you map it to your Today and Tomorrow Teams structure.

Today Teams own Quadrants 1 and 2: Efficiency Engine and Delight in Every Interaction. They are using AI to make the current business better. More efficient operations. Better customer experiences. Clear metrics. Immediate impact.

These are your innovators. They are people who understand the current business deeply and can identify where AI creates leverage. They operate with efficiency and growth mindset. Safe, steady returns. Linear, predictable execution. They are strong planners and organisers.

Tomorrow Teams own Quadrants 3 and 4: AI-Powered Evolution and AI-Born Industries. They are using AI to build what is next. Transformed capabilities. New business models. Longer timeframes. Higher risk and higher potential return.

These are your disruptors. These are people who can imagine fundamentally different approaches. They operate with search and breakthrough mindset. Many bets, few big wins. Fast experiments, fail, learn, adapt cycles. They are explorers thriving in uncertainty.

The Scanner gives both teams clarity about what they are building and how it fits together. Today is not just maintaining the old whilst Tomorrow builds the new. They are both essential, both valuable, both using AI, but in fundamentally different ways.

Using the Scanner for Decision-Making

The real power of the Scanner is not just mapping where you are. It is using it to make decisions about where to invest, what to prioritise, and how to structure your efforts.

When someone proposes an AI initiative, the first question should be: which quadrant does this fit in?

If it is Quadrant 1 or 2, it goes to Today Teams. What is the efficiency gain or customer experience improvement? What is the ROI? How quickly can we implement?

If it is Quadrant 3 or 4, it goes to Tomorrow Teams. What capability or business model are we building? What are we learning? What option does this create? How does this prepare us for future scenarios?

This simple clarity prevents the confusion that paralyses most AI strategies. You are not debating whether an initiative is good or bad. You are clarifying what type of initiative it is and therefore how to evaluate it, resource it, and execute it.

The Scanner also helps you identify gaps. You might discover you are doing lots of Quadrant 1 work but nothing in Quadrant 4. That tells you something important about your strategic stance and where you are vulnerable.

The Resource Allocation Question

One of the questions I get asked constantly is: how do we allocate resources across the quadrants?

There is no universal answer, but here is what I have observed works.

For most established organisations:

40–50% of your AI investment should be in Quadrant 1, Efficiency Engine
20–30% in Quadrant 2, Delight in Every Interaction
15–20% in Quadrant 3, AI-Powered Evolution
10–15% in Quadrant 4, AI-Born Industries

This reflects that Today needs more resources because it is funding everything else. But you are still investing meaningfully in Tomorrow, particularly in transforming your core capabilities.

If you are in a rapidly disrupting industry, you might shift more to Quadrants 3 and 4. If you are in a stable industry, you might concentrate more in Quadrants 1 and 2.

The key is making these allocation decisions consciously based on your strategic stance rather than letting them happen by default.

Avoiding the Complexity Trap

The Scanner's simplicity is its power. Four quadrants. Two dimensions. Clear choices about which quadrant an initiative belongs in and therefore how to approach it.

But I have seen organisations take this simple framework and immediately try to complicate it. They add subquadrants.

They create detailed scoring systems. They build elaborate prioritisation matrices. Do not. The moment you add complexity, you are back to the problem the Scanner was designed to solve.

The framework works precisely because it is simple enough to remember and use without constantly referring to documentation. Every leader in your organisation should be able to sketch the four quadrants from memory and place initiatives into them.

If your people cannot do that, your framework is too complex to actually guide decisions.

The Scanner as Strategic Conversation

The most valuable use of the Scanner is not as a planning tool. It is as a conversation tool.

When your leadership team sits down to discuss AI strategy, put the Scanner on the wall. Ask: where are we investing? Where are we not? Why?

Which quadrant initiatives are succeeding? Which are struggling? What does that tell us?

Are our Today and Tomorrow Teams clear about which quadrants they own? Is there confusion or conflict about who does what?

Are we comfortable with our balance across quadrants given our strategic stance? Or do we need to shift resources?

These conversations create the clarity that enables execution. Not through detailed planning, but through shared understanding of what you are trying to achieve and how the pieces fit together.

Making It Work in Your Context

The Scanner is a framework, not a prescription. You will need to adapt it to your specific context.

Different industries have different opportunities in each quadrant. What Efficiency Engine looks like in healthcare vs. retail vs. manufacturing varies enormously.

Different organisation sizes have different capacities. A start-up might work only in Quadrant 4. A large enterprise needs activity across all four.

Different strategic situations demand different emphasis. If you are defending market position, Quadrants 1 and 2 matter most. If you are trying to disrupt, Quadrants 3 and 4 are critical.

The framework gives you clarity about the types of AI work you could do. Your strategy determines which types you prioritise and how much you invest in each.

The Integration with Today and Tomorrow

Everything we have discussed in this chapter connects directly back to the Today and Tomorrow Teams framework from the previous chapter.

The Scanner does not replace that structure. It enhances it by giving both teams clarity about what they are building.

Today Teams know they own the top half of the Scanner. They are making the current business more efficient and more delightful. They are measured on operational improvements and customer satisfaction. They are innovators working on what exists.

Tomorrow Teams know they own the bottom half of the Scanner. They are transforming capabilities and creating new business models. They are measured on option creation and strategic learning. They are disruptors working on what could exist.

The Scanner becomes the strategic frame that guides what both teams focus on and how they work together. It is the bridge between structure and strategy.

What This Clarity Enables

When I work with organisations that implement both the Today and Tomorrow structure and use the Scanner for strategic clarity, something shifts.

Debates that used to go in circles get resolved quickly. 'Is this initiative Today or Tomorrow work? Which quadrant? Good, now we know how to evaluate it and who should own it'.

Resources get allocated more effectively. Goodbye to every initiative competing on the same criteria. Different quadrants have different success measures.

Teams get energised. They are not confused about their mandate. They know what they are building, why it matters, how it is measured, and how it fits with what others are doing.

Most importantly, execution accelerates. Not because people are working harder, but because they are working with clarity. They know what decisions to make without constantly escalating or coordinating.

That is what good strategy does. It creates clarity that enables distributed decision-making. It allows people throughout the organisation to make good choices aligned with strategic intent without needing constant direction.

The AI Strategy Scanner is not comprehensive. It does not answer every strategic question. It does not eliminate the need for judgement and adaptation.

But it cuts through the overwhelm. It gives you a simple frame for making sense of the AI chaos. It helps you see where you are, where you need to be, and how to get there.

In a domain where complexity is the enemy of execution, that simplicity is worth everything.

The next chapter will address how to actually restructure your organisation to support both Today and Tomorrow work. Because having clear strategy is essential, but it matters only if your organisational design enables you to execute on it.

Structure follows strategy. Let us talk about what structure actually enables adaptability.

9 Leaving the Old City

There is a moment in every real transformation when you begin to realise something quietly confronting, not in a dramatic or cinematic way, but in the slow, dawning way that only real change ever arrives. The old world is not going to disappear overnight, and the new world is not going to arrive fully formed, clean, and ready to move into. It feels much more like leaving a city you have lived in your whole life, a city whose streets you know by heart, whose rhythms you have learned to navigate almost without thinking, whose rules you have mastered so completely that they no longer feel like rules at all. You know how to win here. You know how to survive here. You built your reputation here, your identity, your confidence, your status, your sense of competence, and, in many ways, your sense of self.

This city made you successful. And then, slowly, almost imperceptibly at first, you start to notice something. The ground does not feel as solid as it used to. The infrastructure needs more and more patching. The air feels a little heavier. Things still work, but they take more effort every year, more energy, more force, more control, and more explanation. Nothing is dramatically wrong, and yet something is fundamentally changing.

So you face a choice, even if you do not yet want to admit it to yourself. You can keep optimising life in the old city, getting better and better at a game whose rules are quietly shifting beneath your feet, or you can begin the long, uncomfortable, and deeply personal process of leaving it.

The problem is that leaving a city is never a single decision. It is not a bold announcement, or a strategy deck, or a town hall speech. It is a prolonged, identity-shifting transition, and for a long time you live in an in-between space where you have left what you know but you have not yet mastered what comes next. And in that in-between space, everything in you wants to go back. Your nervous system wants to go back. Your habits want to go back. Your status wants to go back. Your sense of certainty wants to go back. Even if, somewhere deeper inside, you know that the old city is no longer a viable place to build the future.

This is a brutally difficult time to be a leader, not because leaders are failing but because they are being asked to leave a world they mastered and lead into one they have not yet learned how to walk in. There is pressure from boards, pressure from markets, pressure from employees, pressure from brand, pressure from legacy, pressure from payroll, and pressure from reputation, and underneath all of that, there is a very human pressure, the pressure of identity. I see more leaders quietly exhausted, more people taking early retirement, and more people stepping away, not because they do not care but because the cognitive, emotional, and existential load of this transition is immense.

This chapter is not really about strategy. It is about what it actually takes to cross this terrain. Because here is the uncomfortable truth that sits underneath all the frameworks, all the models, and all the good intentions. Even with the right strategy and the right teams, your organisation will still fail unless you redesign how you allocate power, money, and attention. This is the moment where change stops being conceptual and starts becoming real.

In my experience, organisations do not get stuck where people think they do. They do not get stuck primarily in middle management or in bureaucracy or even in process. They get stuck at the top and not because leaders are stupid or uncaring but because the pressure of the role slowly trains you to return to what feels familiar and controllable whenever uncertainty rises.

I once attended a large hotel group conference where the chairman spoke for almost an hour, and about 80% of that time was devoted to numbers, financial performance, margins, growth, cost control, and operational metrics. About 20% was spent on the importance of having the right people, and the last few minutes were reserved for culture. Nothing he said was technically wrong, and yet everything he said revealed the real operating system of the organisation. Money was the centre of gravity, and everything else orbited around it.

This is not a moral failure. It is a human one. The pressure on a CEO is enormous. Your paycheque, your power, your reputation, your track record, your legacy, and your identity are all quietly on the line all the time, and when that pressure increases, most human beings, no matter how intelligent or well intentioned, regress to what feels safe, known, and controllable. Leaders often say they want disruption, but when decisions get uncomfortable, when the outcome is no longer predictable, when the organisation enters genuinely new territory, they unconsciously pull everything back towards the old city.

This is where power actually blocks adaptation.

There is a simple structural truth here, and it is one that many organisations struggle to accept emotionally even when they understand it intellectually. Tomorrow work must never go to committee. If you are in a sinking ship, you do not call back the boats that are out looking for land. You protect them, even if the ship is taking on water, even if the situation is tense, even if it feels unfair, even if every instinct in you wants to pull all resources back to what feels urgent and visible. Just because the current model is under pressure does not mean you abandon the search for what comes next. That is how organisations die with efficiency and dignity.

Money has a similar, and often even stronger, gravitational pull. Most companies are not killed by competitors. They are killed by their own financial logic. I once worked with a bank that proudly showed me their annual report and told me they had three promises, to shareholders, to customers, and to staff. And I remember saying to the leadership team, gently but honestly, this is not true. You have only one promise, and it is to shareholders. If things get tough, you will fire staff and you will squeeze customers, but you will protect shareholder returns, because in your system everything else is negotiable.

They were not bad people. They were simply trapped in a worldview that worships short-term certainty and calls it responsibility. The deeper issue here is not CFOs, and it is not even finance as a function. It is the addiction to shareholder profitability as the only definition of success. Jeff Bezos spent decades training his shareholders not to expect profits but to expect investment, capability building, and long-term optionality, and that was not a financial trick; it was a philosophical stance about what kind of future he was building. Most organisations do the opposite. They optimise for short-term optics and then act surprised when the future never arrives.

If you are serious about building adaptability, Tomorrow funding must be ring-fenced, not just in spreadsheets but in the psychology of the organisation. Because the moment pressure hits (and it always does), finance will want to pull that money back into Today, and if that happens, you are no longer building the future; you are simply managing decline more efficiently.

Exploration is messy, and it looks irresponsible to a system built for optimisation, but that does not make it irresponsible; it simply means you are trying to run two very different logics at the same time.

What leaders pay attention to is just as important as how they allocate power and money, and in many ways it is even more influential, because attention shapes meaning long before it shapes action. Most leadership teams spend most of their time talking about quarterly results and market share, not because these are the most important things but because these are the things they understand, the things they feel competent discussing, and the things that make them feel grounded in a world that is becoming increasingly uncertain. The future gets very little airtime because it feels abstract, ambiguous, and cognitively expensive. It requires leaders to admit that they do not know, and for successful people, that is deeply uncomfortable.

You cannot build an adaptive organisation if leadership attention is permanently trapped in yesterday's scorecards. What leaders consistently talk about becomes what the organisation believes is real, not the strategy deck, not the values poster, but the meeting agenda.

There is another contradiction that sits at the heart of many organisations, and it shows up most clearly in how we measure and reward people. We all say we want adaptability, experimentation, and courage, and then we measure people on quarterly profit, EBITDA, utilisation, and efficiency. We all want to be adaptive, but we reward predictability, and so people do exactly what the system teaches them to do. They protect what works, they minimise risk, they optimise the known, and then we act surprised when nothing truly new ever emerges.

Organisations do not become what they aspire to. They become what they reward.

Underneath all of this, there is a deeper layer that is rarely spoken about, and yet it is the one that drives almost everything. This change threatens who people believe they are. I know this not as a theory, but as something I have lived through in my own life. Earlier in this book, I told you about my years in the restaurant business, about the pace, the ambition, the momentum, and the identity that grows around building and running something that is visibly successful in the world. At that time, my life was filled with restaurants, retail stores, vending machines, and distribution businesses, and without realising it, I had slowly wrapped my entire sense of self around growth, money, movement, and achievement.

And then I lost it all.

In my early thirties, I found myself teaching aerobics, and the fall from one world into another was not just financially difficult; it was emotionally and existentially brutal. It was humiliating. It was shameful. It forced me to let go of a version of myself that I had confused with who I was and to realise, in a way, that only real loss ever teaches you, how tightly we cling to identities that once kept us safe, even when they are no longer who we are becoming.

Rebuilding my life required more than a new plan. It required becoming a different person. Leaders going through this transition are facing the same thing. The fear is not really about being wrong, even though that is what it looks like on the surface. Underneath, it is about identity. Who am I if what made me successful no longer works?

This is why every serious transformation eventually runs into what feels like an organisational immune system. KPIs snap back. Finance tightens. Leadership loses patience. Middle management resists. Culture quietly reasserts itself. Not because people are evil, but because systems, like bodies, are designed to preserve what they know. This is not failure. This is the process. Most organisations do not fail because they chose the wrong strategy. They fail because they lose their nerve in the messy middle.

Change is hard even when the current reality is painful. It is hard to stop eating chocolate after nine o'clock. It is hard to change habits you do not even like. As Joe Dispenza says, people become addicted to lives they do not even enjoy, and the same is true of organisations. You can dislike your business model and still fight to protect it. You can know something is no longer viable and still cling to it, because familiarity feels safer than possibility.

And maybe this is the most honest place to end this chapter, not with a rousing speech or a heroic call to action, but with a quieter recognition of where you actually are right now.

If you are being truthful with yourself, you can probably already feel it. You can feel the old city behind you, still familiar, still comforting, still exhausting. You can feel that something in you already knows you cannot stay, even if another part of you is still negotiating, still delaying, still hoping that a few more optimisations will be enough.

And you can probably also feel the other side, not clearly, not in detail, not as a well-drawn map, but more like a pull, an unease, a sense that something is calling you forward even though you cannot yet fully name it.

This is the hardest part of any real change. Not the decision. Not the execution. The moment before the decision, when you realise that you are no longer who you were, but not yet who you are becoming.

You are standing at the edge of the old city now.

And in that space, a different kind of question begins to form, not 'How do I fix this?' and not even 'What should we do?' It is instead something much more personal and much more confronting.

Who am I willing to become?

10 The Invitation

If you have stayed with this book this far, then somewhere inside you already knows that this was never really a business book in the way most people mean it. It was never about optimising what already exists or squeezing a little more efficiency out of an ageing system or learning a few new tools so you can survive a little longer in the old city. It has always been about a crossing, about that quiet, uncomfortable threshold where something in you already knows that you cannot stay who you are, even if another part of you is still hoping that you can.

At the end of the previous chapter, we arrived at that place together, the place where an old identity no longer quite fits and a new one has not yet fully formed, and that moment, that in-between moment, is always where a deeper kind of change begins. Not the kind that starts with strategy decks and restructuring plans, but the kind that starts with a more personal, more honest, and more confronting realisation, that who you have been, as successful and capable as that version of you may be, is no longer enough for the world that is emerging.

So let me speak to you directly now, not as a futurist and not as a strategist, but simply as another human being who has stood in that same uncertain space in his own life and who has learned, sometimes gently and sometimes painfully, that genuine transformation is never really about technologies or structures or frameworks but about who we become in order to be able to use them wisely.

What sits in front of you now is not a demand; it is an invitation, and it is not only a personal invitation but a collective one.

Because what we are living through right now is not just another cycle of change, not just another disruption, and not just another uncomfortable period that will soon pass and allow things to return to something that feels familiar. We are living through a transition that is as deep and as consequential as the shift out of the agricultural era and then out of the industrial era. Those were not just economic changes. They were changes in how humans understood themselves, how they organised their lives, and how they related to time, to work, to each other, and to meaning itself.

The agricultural era shaped humans who lived by the rhythms of land and season. The industrial era shaped humans who learned to think in terms of machines, efficiency, control, and predictability. We are now being invited to grow beyond that identity as well, not because the industrial way of thinking was wrong but because it has reached the limits of what it can solve.

Just as machines once made human muscle largely irrelevant as a source of value, artificial intelligence is now doing the same thing to much of human cognition. We are already at the point where machines can process information, recognise patterns, and generate solutions faster and more comprehensively than any individual human ever could, and we are only at the very beginning of that curve. Competing with machines on raw thinking power is no longer a meaningful game, in the same way that competing with a steam engine on physical strength stopped being a meaningful game a long time ago.

This does not make humans less important; it makes a different part of us more important.

For a long time, our civilisation has moved from valuing muscle to valuing brain. Now we are being invited into something else entirely, something that is harder to define but impossible to ignore, a shift towards valuing presence, awareness, emotional intelligence, nervous system regulation, intuition, wisdom, creativity, and the quality of consciousness we bring into every situation. Not as a soft, abstract ideal, but as the real foundation of how we make decisions, how we lead, how we build, and how we navigate uncertainty.

In other words, we are being invited into a different way of being human.

This is why your evolution is not separate from your organisation's future. It is the same journey. The inner and the outer are no longer separable. The state from which you lead, the quality of awareness you bring into conversations, the way your nervous system responds to pressure and uncertainty, the stories you tell yourself about who you are and what you are capable of – all of these now shape outcomes more than any strategy document ever could.

For a long time, leadership was about having answers. About projecting certainty. About being the smartest person in the room. In the world that is emerging, leadership is becoming something quite different. It is becoming about holding uncertainty without collapsing into fear. About asking better questions rather than rushing to premature answers. About creating space for others rather than filling every silence with your own thinking. About being grounded enough inside yourself that you do not need to control everything outside yourself.

This is not a small shift and it is not an optional one.

The future is not waiting for us to feel ready. It is already here, and it will increasingly reward those who can stay present, adaptive, and creatively responsive in the face of complexity, rather than those who cling to certainty and control in a world that no longer supports either.

So this is the invitation. Not to work harder. Not to become more efficient inside a system that is already fading.

But to evolve.

To become the kind of human being who can live and lead in a world where certainty is no longer the currency, where intelligence is no longer the differentiator, and where your inner state increasingly determines the quality of your decisions, your relationships, and your impact.

It is an invitation to do the inner work, not because it is fashionable but because without it the outer work will always collapse back into old patterns. It is an invitation to build Tomorrow, not as a side project but as a real commitment to the future. It is an invitation to use the tools and frameworks you now have, not as mechanical checklists but as expressions of a deeper shift in how you see, think, and choose.

Perhaps most of all, it is an invitation to loosen your grip on the identity that once made you successful and to allow yourself to become a beginner again, to step into uncertainty without needing to pretend you already know how everything will turn out, to trust that a more spacious, more conscious, and more human way of leading is not a weakness in the world that is coming but its greatest strength.

I am not promising that this path is easy. Real evolution never is. It will ask you to question things you have built your sense of self around. It will ask you to sit with discomfort rather than immediately trying to control or fix it. It will ask you to let go of versions of yourself that once served you well but that now quietly limit what you are able to become.

But I am promising you this.

On the other side of this work is not just a more adaptable organisation but a different quality of life. Less reactivity. Less exhaustion. More clarity. More presence. More meaning. And a deeper sense that you are no longer fighting the future but learning how to move with it.

We have reached the end of this book, but if you are honest with yourself, you will know that what is really ending here is not a reading experience but a certain way of seeing yourself and your role in the world.

And what begins from here is not a project. It is a journey. An ongoing, imperfect, deeply human journey of becoming.

The invitation is simple. Not easy. But simple. To step forward. To keep walking.

And to allow yourself, and the people and organisations you lead, to become something new.

Index